WHEN LIFE HANDS YOU LEMONS, PUCKER UP AND SING!

My Journey from Tragedy to Transformation

Cathy Lynn Massengale

WHEN LIFE HANDS YOU LEMONS, PUCKER UP AND SING!
My Journey from Tragedy to Transformation

Disclaimers:
This is a work of nonfiction. The events in this book are portrayed to be the best of Cathy Lynn Massengale's memory. While all the stories in this book are true, some names and identifying details have been changed to protect the privacy of the people involved.

ISBN: 978-1523278848

Cover Design by Ranilo Cabo *with creative inspiration provided by* Holly Holt, Southern Muse Services
Layout and typesetting: Ranilo Cabo
Copyediting by Camille DeSalme, *www.AnEyeforEditing.com*
Book Midwife: Carrie Jareed

Printed in the United States of America

WHEN LIFE
HANDSYOU
LEMONS,
PUCKER UP
AND SING!

Credits and Acknowledgments

I would like to express my gratitude to the many people who saw me through this book; to all those who provided support, talked things over, read, wrote, offered comments, allowed me to quote their remarks and assisted in the editing, proofreading and design. I beg forgiveness of all those who have been with me over the course of the years and whose names I have failed to mention.

Bob Sima – *www.bobsima.com*
Karen Drucker – *www.karendrucker.com*
Gentle Thunder – *www.1gentlethunder.com*
Bart Smyth - *www.amoderndayshaman.net*
Iris Bolton
Debbie Loshbough
Kelly Massengale Pierce
Christy Massengale Olesen

This book is dedicated to my Father who
Taught me how to appreciate and love music
among many other qualities;
And my Mother who
Taught me to be strong and determined,
With all my love.

CONTENTS

PREFACE

I have never written a book before and I have never thought of myself as a writer, but the feeling came over me one afternoon while I was sitting on the screen porch of my mother's house that this was a story I was supposed to write and share with the world so that it might bring its readers hope and comfort during a tragedy or a difficult journey.

I was blessed to have wonderful, loving parents and a loving childhood. However, my life on the road to and through adulthood has been filled with hard-to-overcome challenges and difficult experiences. For reasons that are not clear to me, I have been able to survive, stay strong and keep going and ultimately memorialize my journey to share with you. Today I feel a deep sense of love and gratitude that comes from choosing the road to love, faith and forgiveness rather than choosing fear, anger and resentment. I do believe it is a choice.

This book contains descriptions of quite emotional experiences some of you will find difficult to read. It's important for you to know that I share my story for the sole purpose of helping others to survive any similar circumstance or situation. My desire is that my story will bring you hope to never give up, because the darkness will pass. This is a story of surviving loss in general and, specifically, my family's mental illness, divorce, domestic violence, drug addiction, alcoholism, murder/suicide, unexpected death of loved ones, and more. It is my sincerest desire that when you finish reading it you will feel hopeful and comforted in the knowledge that you too can survive any trauma that has led you down a dark path or just led you to read this book. I have come to believe that my purpose in life is to testify to the world that we can find happiness and forgiveness even in the face of evil, destruction and despair.

I did not do everything right in my life, far from it, but I believe that for whatever reason, this was supposed to be my life and there were no coincidences—that it has all happened for a reason. By divine selection I was born into the family I grew up with and by divine selection I was to be the mother of my children and Nana to my grandchildren. Because of my faith I was able to move past the "why me" mind-set and actually feel blessed that my journey has brought me to the place I am today. My journey is not over and I cannot wait to see what the universe has in store for me next.

My biggest wish is that you find your inner peace and never give up.

Peace, love and light to all.

Cathy

CHAPTER 1

My Family

I was sitting in a chair on the screen porch of my mom's house, looking out over the beautiful view of Lake Lanier. The house sits on a small cove and I looked out over our double-decker dock and noticed that boats were slowly cruising along the cove, making their way to the biggest part of the lake beyond the cove. It was a warm sunny day at the end of May 2014. My mind was wandering as I realized how surreal it felt to be alone in this huge lake house after the tragedy that had happened here and the aftermath that was still ongoing at the time.

It was the first time the house had been completely empty of people, furniture, families and activities in thirty years. I was lost in the memories of hours spent with my mother, my kids and my sisters on that porch, sitting at the glass table, smoking, talking, drinking, eating, laughing, joking, reminiscing about childhood times, and just being silly, which was one of our favorite things to do. My mother could be a lot of fun but she also had a stern and somewhat judgmental side. She never pulled any punches with you; if she thought it, she said it. She didn't have much of a filter, even when she was younger. She was pragmatic, a strong woman who almost always stood her ground with her husbands and her children.

My mother was a beautiful woman who had been a great parent when we were kids. I am the oldest of three girls, our entire family was born in Texas. My parents met in college in Dallas and married in September 1953 and I was born thirteen months later.

My paternal grandfather was a Methodist minister and my paternal grandmother was a teacher. We lived very close to them in Texas. When they moved to Oklahoma City, when I was about four years old, we packed up and moved there, too, and my parents bought their first home. I remember that as a child I didn't much like living in OKC. I didn't have many friends and I remember getting picked on a lot in school by a girl who liked to bully me. I felt hollow and lonely inside, as if I didn't fit in, so I was very withdrawn. What I did like about living there was being close to Colorado. My grandfather had bought a piece of land in Woodland Park, Colorado. He and Dad—along with other family members—built a small two-bedroom cabin there which our whole family loved to visit. The five of us would drive to that cabin most summers and many school holidays for vacations. We loved the pine trees that surrounded the cabin, the hummingbirds, the snow and the mountain views. It was such a peaceful place and we all sensed the closeness and comfort that surrounded our family when we were there, especially our father. In the summer, we went to the rodeo and rode horses on the trail rides in our new jeans and cowboy hats we bought at The Cowhand Shop on Main Street. The shop is still there, owned by the same family that owned it when we were kids.

Dad liked to drive us up to the top of Pikes Peak. In those days the road was still gravel and looking out the windows was a little scary, so he took every hairpin curve at about five mph. It probably took us hours to get to the top. In some places the car would get pretty close to the edge of a drop-off, which scared my mother to the point that she would have to get down on the floorboard of the front seat so she couldn't see out the window. The three of us would laugh till we cried, watching her. We loved going up to the top of that mountain. You could see farther away than from any other place we had ever been. In the summer our tradition was to go to the North Pole, a theme park on the road to the top of the Peak. We have such great memories of those times with our parents and grandparents. Later in my life I would take my kids and grandchildren to the same North Pole on that road going up Pikes Peak.

When my sisters and I were young we spent a lot of time with our grandparents and we loved being with them. They taught us so much about life and what it meant to be part of a loving family. You could just feel how much love they had for their children, and the love they had for us, their grandchildren. It made me feel incredibly safe as a child being surrounded by that much love. They taught us to respect them and others, imparted good morals and values, made us use manners and showed us how to have a good sense of humor. Grandfather liked to tell jokes in his sermons and he easily made people laugh. I have a memory from childhood of standing up in the pew in the middle of his sermon and yelled at the top of my lungs, "Hi Paw-Paw." I must have been about six or seven years old. I remember feeling his immediate embarrassment, and I'm sure my father was horrified. But Grandfather recovered quickly, using his wonderful humor by introducing me to the congregation, then he told a joke. He liked to use humor to make people feel comfortable in awkward moments. I always remember that about him. My father had the same ability to crack a joke and make people laugh and feel comfortable.

My parents and grandparents really loved music. My grandparents had a stereo that used a reel-to-reel tape player hidden in a desk drawer in the kitchen. Another desk drawer contained a turntable that was connected to speakers mounted in the corners of the living room, so when you sat anywhere in the room the stereo sounds pointed directly at you. They played mostly music from movie musicals. I especially remember the music from *South Pacific* playing frequently. They adored the stories the music told as well as just listening to the music. Thinking back on it, it was a pretty progressive stereo setup for the early 1960s.

My grandmother had a sewing machine. She taught me to sew by hand and by machine. It was the kind with a pedal you put both feet on and pumped back and forth to make the needle go up and down. She also taught me to crochet, though I don't remember how to any more. As a young adult, I made clothes for myself and my baby daughter and my grandmother made my daughter's crib bedding out of yellow roses and yellow gingham. Her whole bedroom was decorated with the yellow-roses-and-gingham theme. I still have the comforter and used it when my grandchildren were born, her great-grandchildren. In fact, my fifteen-year-old grandson loves that comforter and it will be passed on to him as a family heirloom.

Dad was the oldest of three children. He had two sisters, and we all lived in Oklahoma until one sister got married and moved to Missouri. I was pretty close to my aunts when I was younger, and I have felt pretty close to Dad's middle sister most of my life. They always gave me such affectionate attention. Something warm about their spirits made me feel very comforted and appreciated. After my aunt LuAnn and her husband moved away, Dad would send me to visit them by putting me on a Greyhound bus. I was fairly young, and you couldn't do that today. I adored those trips and cherished spending time with them, and I learned to enjoy travel and adventure from those trips alone.

My sisters and I make an effort to stay in contact with family, though it's hard because we are spread out all over the US and some are in Europe. Family was very important to Dad and to his parents. He truly loved his nieces and nephews and enjoyed spending time with them—and they adored him.

We never knew our mother's family. They all lived in Texas. We spent a large part of our lives trying to figure out why she was not close to her brother and never lived with him and why her mother's mother, "Nanny," raised her rather than her own parents raising her. We found out later in life that her parents divorced when Mom was two years old, not a common thing in Texas in 1934. Mom struggled with knowing, or not knowing, how to have a successful relationship with men because she never experienced or witnessed a successful relationship between her parents or in their family as a whole. I believe she treasured having us three girls to take care of, and she doted on us the way she probably always wished she had been doted on as a child. I think loving us may have been the closest thing to knowing what if felt like to feel affection and show love to her family. I doubt she had ever experienced real love in relationships with men because it was conditional on what she needed from them.

There are three-and-half years between my younger sister Kelly and me, and fifteen months after Kelly was born came my baby sister, Christy. We were "stair-step" sisters. Mom loved to dress us up at Easter and take lots of pictures. She would roll our hair in bobby-pin curls so we had that '50s hairdo. I think she loved being a mom, but she wanted us to be able to stand up for ourselves when we got older rather than only relying on other people. I remember my childhood fondly; nothing bad or traumatic happened to me that I recall. I always felt cherished and nurtured by both of my parents and by my grandparents.

My parents built their second house in Oklahoma City when I was in the third grade. My mother spent numerous hours thinking of cute and decorative ways to make it beautiful and homey. In my bedroom, she put wallpaper on the ceiling (a wide blue-and-white stripe), painted the walls and put up a floral border matching the ceiling wallpaper at the top of the walls. She made sure we all had built-in desks for our homework. She had a great eye for decorating and it was passed on to my sister Kelly. I like to think I got a little of it, too.

Dad had a great ear for music and played drums when he was a teenager. He even made a demo record in the '40s on a 78-speed vinyl record. His demo had a song called "Change That Lock" on side A; side B was "Hey! Ba-Ba-Re-Bop." When

I was six years old I remember him playing that record on our hi-fi system; we couldn't afford a stereo yet. Dad was a fan of all kinds of music and absolutely loved the Beatles. In 1964, after the first Beatles album was released in America, he bought all their singles and albums and even brought home Beatles wallpaper one day. The eyes of our entire family was glued to our black and white television set to watch the first Beatles performance in the United States live on The Ed Sullivan Show.

In the '50s and '60s, my whole family watched variety shows. We would gather around our console black-and-white television waiting for *The Wonderful World of Disney* on Sunday nights. We also watched Dinah Shore, Andy Williams, Doris Day, Perry Como, Ed Sullivan, and Judy Garland, to name a few of our favorites. In hindsight, I think it's safe to say that, when I was growing up, watching these wonderful entertainers sing, dance and perform on television were some of our happiest family time together. I would get excited anticipating the singing and laughter the music created in our living room. Dad would almost be giddy watching the performers' belt out the songs of the day. It was so inspiring to me and it would play a major role in each of our lives as we grew up and in our connection to music.

When I was five or six and living in our first house in Oklahoma City, my grandparents gave us their black upright grand piano in hopes one or all of us girls would take piano lessons and learn to play it. The keyboard cover said it was a Vough and was made in 1900. The only place we had to put it was in my bedroom. My mom would play that piano and sing the songs she had learned in her childhood. She could read music. She couldn't play by ear but recalled how to play the songs she'd learned and memorized as a child. One of the songs she used to play well was "Santa Lucia" and she played and sang it frequently.

Mom and Dad took us to see all the movie musicals as soon as they were released in the theaters. We saw *The Music Man*, *The Sound of Music*, *South Pacific*, *Funny Girl*, *Mary Poppins*, *Chitty Chitty Bang Bang*, and so many others. Then they would buy the album soundtracks and my sisters and I would sing along and learn all the lyrics and act out the performances. As small children we would perform various songs from *The Sound of Music*, *The Music Man* and *Mary Poppins* on the hearth in front of my grandparents' fireplace when we went to visit them. I specifically remember the numerous performances we did of the "So Long, Farewell" scene from *The Sound of Music*. My baby sister, Christy, even looked a little bit like "Gretl"— at least in my ten-years-old mind. Julie Andrews would have been so proud of us; I'm sure of it. Our parents loved it and our grandparents encouraged our mini-performances every time we got together.

My cousins would sometimes join in too. My dad's sister (Aunt Gwynne, with the beautiful voice) would play "Edelweiss" on the guitar and we would all sing along just as in the movie—at least in our minds. These are such great memories of times together pretending we were going to be the next entertainment stars of the world.

It's no surprise that I grew up singing all the time and was so inspired by Barbra Streisand in the movie *Funny Girl* that I knew early on I wanted to be a singer. Since my childhood I've admired this woman for her amazing voice and her brilliant acting abilities. Today I also admire her humanitarian efforts. I distinctly remember thinking as a teenager that being a singer was an unrealistic desire, but I thought I had a good voice so it became a secret dream. When I was a senior in high school, Dad bought me a guitar and we bought a *Mel Bay's Guitar Chords* book. I taught myself to play the chords and I sang songs with my favorite records of Joni Mitchell, Judy Collins, Joan Baez, Pete Seeger, Crosby, Stills & Nash, James Taylor, Bob Dylan, Peter, Paul and Mary, and Linda Ronstadt, among others. I also learned to play and sing a lot of traditional folk songs, things you could sing around a camp fire or with a group of friends. I wanted to make sure I had other skills, in case music didn't pan out for me, so I took typing and shorthand in my senior year and my first year in college, which turned out to serve me well in pretty much every job I had in the future.

CHAPTER 2

The Family Breakup

When I was in the ninth grade, in 1968, Dad got a new job and we moved to Concord, California. It would be the last time we lived in the same city as my grandparents. It was a really good move for me because I made a number of close friends and became much more outgoing. I feel lucky to have grown up in the '50s and '60s, because I've always felt I belonged in that era.

Dad took me to San Francisco and let me ride the trolleys, alone, while he was in a business meeting. It was great fun. Also in 1968, he took me to the intersection of Haight St. and Ashbury St. It was the height of the hippie culture. I watched them walking up and down the streets and saw many carrying guitars and singing on street corners. A sea of young people with flowers in their long hair. It really made an impact on me and I decided I wanted to be cool. Then at the end of ninth grade, just as I had become a wannabe hippie, Dad got another transfer and moved us to

Georgia, to a suburb in North Atlanta. I was terribly upset to leave California where it felt so progressive to move to what I thought was going to be a backwoods, southern, confederate flag waving state.

In large part the move was because Mom was never happy in California (Dad and I loved it). She had no social life and didn't work outside the home so she was very lonely. Dad was a traveling salesman, gone during the week. Mom started drinking more frequently about that time. I guess it helped her avoid her loneliness. I do remember coming home from school to find her locked in her room on a regular basis, which she only did when she was drinking.

Dad worked hard and tried his best to provide for his family. If they had any financial problems, they kept it a secret from us. Therefore, it seemed to us that we never needed or wanted anything he and Mom couldn't provide, though they didn't provide everything we wanted.

My sisters got into horses soon after moving to Georgia. They had horses, rode horses, showed horses, and practically lived at the barn after school.

Mom had been very athletic in high school. She had been a cheerleader, water skier, and swimmer and had been very active in other outside sports. She had ridden horses in rodeos in Austin, Texas when she was a kid and had ridden in the barrel races. She loved doing horse activities with my sisters, such as taking them to horse shows for competition. Mom never let any of us feel sorry for ourselves when we didn't win a ribbon or when things didn't go our way. She taught us how to be good sports when we lost at something. She liked to tell us to pull ourselves up with our bootstraps and carry on with life, to be positive. She was down-to-earth and didn't tolerate a lot of whining or nonsense.

When I was a teenager, my parents put pressure on me to be the example. When I would leave the house to go out with friends, Dad used to tell me, "Be a lady." I was a pretty good kid. They trusted me more than most parents I knew trusted their kids, and they treated me with respect. All my friends growing up loved to hang out at my house and loved my parents. Mom was a great homemaker and a great cook, loved to decorate, and loved the holidays (Christmas was her favorite). Our home was always beautiful, clean and comfortable. At times, it seemed she could even be childlike, as if she could easily connect to her inner child. I say that because I've always had this feeling Mom did not have the chance to enjoy being a child, but it's speculation on my part. She never told us much about her life as a child, but she would get down on the floor and play with us and our dolls as if she were just another kid.

When I was a senior in high school, Mom decided to get a job and earn her own income. My sisters and I had noticed much more fighting going on between her and my dad. As we got older, I think she was bored staying home all day and wanted more. Dad had always been gone during the week. Unfortunately, Dad wanted her to stay at home but she was ready for a new life. She took a realtor course and soon got her license to sell real estate. She started to thrive in the working world and became a little wild. She probably had a midlife crisis. This was her first taste of freedom: she made her own money and could do what she wanted with it. I think that after she sold her first house she knew she wanted out of the marriage. I can't speak for my sisters but I wasn't surprised when she told us she was filing for divorce. It was pretty devastating to us and to our father. Our lives changed significantly after their split. We suddenly became a "broken family." That was to have damaging effects on each of us kids as we continued to grow up; we each have different perspectives on how that hurt us.

I went right into college after high school and moved into an apartment that I shared with two other girls. It was close to the community college I attended, which worked out well. My parents' divorce was highly contentious at that point and Dad was extremely emotional. Mom seemed to be drinking more. To make matters worse, she began a relationship with another man. It was hard to watch my family fall apart, but I knew I needed to focus on my college courses and devote my time and attention to school.

One day, standing in the registration line for my college courses, I made an on-the-spot decision to change my major to music with voice as my instrument. This felt so right—but then I had to audition in front of the voice faculty of the music department and I had to pick a classical song to sing. Well, I had no idea what to sing, so I chose the only one I knew. I chose the song my mom used to sing when she played the piano when I was a child. You guessed it…"Santa Lucia"…and the looks on the faculty faces were "Really?"

Then they asked what other songs I knew. I knew numerous songs from musicals and without any sheet music whatsoever, I sang the songs I knew by heart.

They loved it.

Suddenly, I was a music major with voice as my instrument and piano as a secondary major. For the next three years I worked incredibly hard and sang in all the musical productions produced by DeKalb College (now Georgia Perimeter College) Music Department. It was wonderful and magical. I absolutely loved my teachers, professors and my time there.

I also learned a lot of discipline and dedication to learning and improving my skill. I spent countless hours in the practice rooms studying and practicing piano and singing, but I utterly adored every minute of it.

It also distracted me from the sadness and heartbreak of what was happening to my parents while they fought each other over money and possessions.

CHAPTER 3

The Crystal Pistol Show

My sister Kelly was working in Atlanta restaurants around this time and Christy was accepted into an equine school in Oklahoma where our grandparents still lived, so each of us went our separate ways. It was the '70s and while Mom was struggling to make it as a realtor (not a good time for real estate sales in Atlanta) she was also moving forward with the divorce. Dad was very distraught over what was going on with their legal battle. He was sad and lonely and looking for love and companionship, which he found in a younger woman he would marry soon after the divorce was final. That didn't last very long, and he was alone again.

Mom had some wild oats that being single again brought on pretty quickly. It didn't take her long to hook up with a younger man, which made sense to me because she was always young at heart. She had really turned into a party girl, a "let's just have fun" girl. Even though she could not hold her liquor (two highballs and she was blitzed) she kept drinking. She could not keep up with the real drinkers. She and her younger "beau" liked to smoke pot. She could manage that a little better than the booze, but it was pretty weird watching Mom turn into the party and pot-smoking girl when I was eighteen years old. She and her younger man managed to stay together for the next fourteen years.

At that time I was still living in the apartment close to college. I met a guy in the music department, a percussionist who also played guitar and sang. We started singing and playing as a duo, performing around the North Atlanta area. We did that for several years while going to music school. We played at coffeehouses, cafés, and the Steak and Ale restaurants and fine-dining restaurants popular in the late '70s. But I really wanted to get into performing in musical shows in town. So I had some head shots made and listed all my singing performances and the roles I had been in over the last several years at college and started looking for places to audition.

I heard about an audition for the Crystal Pistol show at Six Flags Over Georgia. In that show, singers and dancers performed songs from famous musicals and Broadway shows at the Six Flags Theater, with a live orchestra, four or five nights a week. I had never considered myself to be a dancer but it looked like a great opportunity for a singer. Some other voice students were going to audition; I figured I didn't have anything to lose and went with them. I'll never forget the song I sang at audition: "The Way We Were," from the movie with the same name. Well, lo and behold...I got a callback. For that audition, they told me the song they wanted me to sing, "Delta Dawn," made famous by Tanya Tucker in 1972.

After the singing audition, we were going to have to do a dance audition. Oh boy, I was thinking, that'll be the end of me, so I decided to just do my best. After I sang at my audition, they put us in groups, taught us a five-minute dance routine, and gave us an hour or so to practice. Then we did our dance audition, in groups, while the judges scored us. It wasn't that difficult and I was actually able to keep up with everyone. A couple of girls from school—one was my friend—had also made it that far. After we were done they told us to go home, saying they would call the ones who made it into the show, along with five alternates. We were told the alternates would learn all the songs and routines so they could sub if anyone were to drop out of the show.

I went with the two girls from school to my friend's house to sit and wait for the call—we had all provided her telephone number so we'd get the call at the same place. One girl got the call pretty quickly; she was "in." Then the other got the call "in." Last but not least, I got the call. I had been selected as an alternate, and they would be in contact with me as to when I should go to rehearsal. The other girls would start rehearsal immediately. Well, even though I was very proud of myself for making it that far, I was pretty disappointed because my friends were going to be in the show and I figured that was the end of that.

The summer before, I had auditioned at Manhattan School of Music in New York City. I'd gone with a friend and we both auditioned, but I did not get accepted and he did. I had been planning for a year to audition again for that same conservatory. I was determined to get into that school. I had decided to go back to the community college and continue to work on my voice for another year then try again at the next auditions, which were in the summer of the Crystal Pistol auditions.

When it was time to go back to NYC to try again for acceptance to the conservatory, I got an offer from my friend who had been accepted to the school the prior summer. He knew I was going back to that summer's auditions, so he invited me to move into the house he was living in. He was house-sitting for a family who wanted someone to watch their large home in Brooklyn Heights rather than leaving it empty. This friend was an ex-boyfriend and he wanted me to move to NYC as soon as school was out for the summer. He suggested I look for a summer job. He said he was sure I would be accepted to the school, and I would love New York City, and the house had many bedrooms and lots of room to move around. It did sound pretty exciting. So after finding out I was not going to start rehearsal for the Crystal Pistol show, I decided to take him up on his offer.

My father and mother were also supportive of my decision, but they were fighting over the divorce settlement at that moment and that's where all their energies were being directed. My father was really upset with my mother's attorney, who was milking every dollar he could find out of Dad. The animosity between them was gut-wrenching, and Dad had visited me at my apartment several times, where he ended up crying his eyes out over the breakup of his family. It was quite devastating to me as well, and I found it unbearable and excruciating to watch him break down like that. Even though their legal case was causing him such pain, he understood my

New York opportunity was a great one. Thankfully, he gave me his blessing and said he would help however he could.

First, I had to move out of my rented apartment room. While I was literally packing up my things and waiting for the movers to come and load up my bedroom furniture and my piano (the one my grandparents gave us as children) to move it back to my parent's house, I got "the call" I wasn't expecting. It was Six Flags telling me someone had dropped out of the show and as the next alternate I was now needed to start rehearsals the next day.

Really?

Well, I told them I had made other plans and was moving to New York City to go to conservatory the next day. I ended up driving to Manhattan for that second audition, and I stayed there and lived in that house in Brooklyn and began looking for a summer job. It was free so I really didn't see any reason not to go for it.

That was such a crossroads in my life, and I've often wondered if anything would have turned out differently for me if I had taken that job. I left the next day for the big city and an exciting new life.

CHAPTER 4

Welcome to New York City

I selected a really difficult aria to sing at my audition. I thought about how different this audition was going to be from my first audition, the one to get into the music department at the community college, when I sang "Santa Lucia." The aria is "Mon coeur s'oeuvre à ta voix," from the opera *Samson and Delilah*. My singing it was a culmination of the past three years of voice lessons, hard work and constant practice. I felt really good about it when I was done singing and was very proud of myself, so I kept my fingers crossed that I had made it this time. I learned within a few days that I had been accepted to the school. I was so excited that I had accomplished one of the biggest dreams of my life. Now I was living in that house in Brooklyn Heights with my old boyfriend, in an entirely new city with new surroundings; and I was really excited about the possibilities.

I was nineteen years old and fearless. Nothing could stop me. Soon after my arrival, after getting settled into my new home, I decided to go into the city and try to find a job. I put on a dress and took the subway into Manhattan and started walking around Midtown. I stopped at a phone booth to look up temporary employment agencies in the Yellow Pages. I called one close by and they told me to come right in. So I did and was interviewed. Then I was sent out immediately for a job interview as a receptionist with a talent agency on East 59th Street and Lexington Avenue. I could type, take shorthand, and had a little experience helping at my dad's office. They talked to me and hired me on the spot. I actually started working that day. I couldn't believe my incredible luck to find a job in New York City within a few hours. It was a really exciting job; as receptionist, I screened all the calls and controlled which people got in to see the agents for the first time. I ended up meeting a ton of actors and all the commercial stars of the day. I even met Alan Alda.

It wasn't fun riding the subway for an hour into town from Brooklyn and back at the end of the day. I had to wear a dress to work, and during rush hour commuters were packed on the subway like sardines. I frequently got molested by hands coming up my skirt, but I couldn't tell whose hand it was. I loved the job but the subway ride was bad.

It wasn't long before the ex-boyfriend and I started up a relationship again, which eventually led to my first experience with domestic violence. He became extremely controlling and decided he didn't like it when I left the cap off the toothpaste tube or when I didn't put my shoes neatly in the closet at night. He would become enraged at such little things that I could never figure out what I needed to do to stop triggering his anger. At the time, I thought it was my fault. I really tried hard not to do anything to make him angry, but it was impossible.

One of his friends had been flirting with me at a party we had attended; and even though I was not interested in him, it seemed to set off a pattern of jealousy that I did not understand.

Then one day he was so mad he threw me up against the wall and started screaming at me and telling me I was to blame for his anger. He said if I would just stop doing this or that then he wouldn't get mad. I don't even remember anymore what he specified; yet now I know this is typical behavior from men who batter. I realized that it didn't matter what I did: I wasn't in control of whether he hit or pushed me. I learned that he needed to take responsibility for his anger and that it was not my fault.

Young and excited about where my life was going, I was lucky I had the courage to decide pretty quickly that I was having none of that anger and violence in my life. I realized that I didn't need him or the drama. So after trying once, unsuccessfully, to leave, I ended up sneaking out of that house in the middle of the night. I loaded up my car and drove into NYC to a women's hotel close to Midtown. That's when I found out having a car in Manhattan was not a good idea at all. It was the middle of the night, I was traumatized from all the emotions of having to escape that situation, so I parked on the street in front of the hotel just to go to the front desk to check in. I was gone less than ten minutes and when I got back to my car…it was gone. I was sure someone had stolen it so I called the police. They told me nope, it had been impounded and it was at their impound lot with a ticket for illegal parking.

Wow, that was quick. I learned a hard lesson that night and after getting my car back, I never did that again.

Luckily, that boyfriend did not stalk or pursue me. He didn't come looking for me or try to apologize or any of that. I knew we were done and there was no need to try again. There was only keeping my eye on the prize…and he wasn't it.

I was really upset with myself and wondered how I let it get that extreme before leaving. In hindsight, I actually don't think two months was that long to realize it was no good and I needed to get out. In reaction to that experience, I went through a period of "hating men." So I started paying closer attention to women. I was definitely confused and thinking maybe I was a lesbian or possibly bisexual. I had no interest in a relationship with any male. It was also very trendy to be gay in the Upper West Side of Manhattan in the mid-'70s, and many of my girlfriends and I liked to go to gay bars, dance, and have fun. That protected us from being hit on by men, which made it more enjoyable. I'm not saying being gay is a choice, I don't believe it is. I do think we all go through some form of reckoning about our own sexual identity at some point in our lives. In my case, my experience with domestic violence caused me to turn away from men. It didn't last long and helped me to feel confident in my eventual evaluation regarding my own sexual preference, that of being heterosexual.

After leaving that house in Brooklyn, I suddenly found myself without a place to live and I couldn't move into my dormitory until school started. That was a month away. Then I met the man who managed the front desk of that dormitory. Because school had not started yet, the building was empty.

He was nice enough to let me sleep in a janitor's room in the basement, unofficially, and I lived there until I was assigned a dorm room.

I resolved the car problem, too. I would park it around the Riverside Church area until my dad flew up and drove it home for me.

Soon I was meeting other musicians and women in my dormitory who played guitars and sang. We started a little band, a trio. We'd each pick out songs to sing and learn them with each other in three-part harmony. Before too long, we had a full set of cover songs we could play for people. We started playing everywhere we could. In the halls, our dorm rooms, the common dorm areas, and all around that college district, until we had our own little following of fans. We played at coffee shops and taverns and anywhere we could find. It was probably the most fun and memorable time of my life. Plus, I really loved my partners; we had a wonderful friendship.

We played a concert one night that included about twelve songs. Someone in the audience recorded it on a small, portable, cassette tape player. It's not very good quality but you could tell we sounded really good. After I moved back to Georgia I soon lost contact with those women, but thirty-five years later, with the use of social media, I was able to find one of them and we reconnected. It was interesting to learn she had been looking for me for years. She'd had that cassette tape of our concert put on a compact disc and she wanted to mail a copy of the disc to me. It was really great to reconnect with her and have a recording of our music from that time in my life. I am so glad our paths crossed when they did. We had so much fun.

When school at the conservatory started, I had to take a placement test for music theory. I absolutely loved music theory and had the greatest theory teacher at that little college in Georgia. His name was Dr. Edward Lormand and he knew how to make learning exciting and make you want to work for it. For our final grade and before we could get our credit, we each had to prepare a piano reduction. He assigned each student three hundred continual measures from well-known orchestral pieces (everyone got a different piece). You had to reduce the measures, with all the orchestral instruments' parts, to a piano score. He used the best piano majors to play your piece upon its completion. It was really hard, but it was really fun. He was so good and I'd learned so well that when I took my placement test for theory at the conservatory, I was exempted from that subject because I could identify a German augmented sixth chord in an oral exam: I didn't have to take any more theory classes.

I did have to take a counterpoint class. It wasn't nearly as fun as Dr. Lormand's class. I was assigned a voice teacher who was somewhat snobby and condescending. I hoped it would get better with her, but it didn't and that was a massive disappointment.

After all the buildup and excitement of getting into that school, I eventually became disillusioned with the school and questioned where I wanted to go with my music and singing. Although I had so much fun with the people there and the things we could do in NYC, I realized I really didn't have the voice to sing opera at the caliber of, and among competition of, classically trained singers in that city. At the end of the year, my heart wasn't really into pursuing the life of an opera singer anymore. I knew I was good at singing popular and folk music and harmonizing with others, which is what I really loved and wanted to do. That's when I decided to go back to Atlanta to continue performing as a duo with my old singing partner. On top of that, the divorce had cleaned Dad out financially and he told me he didn't have the money for tuition. I could have applied for financial aid, but it didn't seem like my right path at that time.

I returned to Atlanta and continued playing music around there with my duo partner until he met a woman, fell in love and got married. It turned out that she expected him to end his friendship with me, which he did. This discontinued our friendship and singing relationship for many years.

That's when I started looking for my next singing partner. One night I had gone out on the town with some friends to a bar. A band was playing and I noticed that one of the guitar players sounded really good and when I looked closer, I realized I knew him. Randall and I had been in the same high school graduating class. We'd graduated four years prior. I also remembered he'd had a band in high school, too. During his break, he came over, having recognized me, and started talking to me. I began telling him what I had been doing the last four years and told him I was looking for my next singing partner. "Well, that's interesting," he said. "My band is looking for a singer." His band had two guitar players, a bass player, and a drummer. Randall told me the type of cover songs they were focused on, a pretty good mixture of music, and that he had a few originals. He played slide guitar and his roots were definitely in the blues. Not my regular genre of music for singing, but they were playing stuff I knew I could sing. I told him I might be interested and he said to come and audition. A few days later, I did.

When I arrived the whole band was there and set up, ready to play. I told Randall to just play any Linda Ronstadt song and suggested a couple. He knew "Desperado" so off we went. When it was over, he looked at me and said, "Wow, you've got a good voice." We played for another hour. He sang a few songs. I harmonized with him and he harmonized with me. It fell together easily and naturally—it sounded good and it felt good. He was a phenomenal lead guitar player and the guys in the band all seemed excited and pleased with the sound, too.

Randall asked if I was interested in joining the band, and I said yes. The next day he went to the bank for the first time in his life and applied for a loan to purchase a really nice PA (public address) system, with new microphones and microphone stands. He already had some gigs booked so we were off and running. Now I'm a singer in a rock-'n'-roll band, something new and different for the next stage of my life.

CHAPTER 5

"Mommy, the couch is on fire!"

We had a pretty successful band. We got an agent and played in a ton of bars in the city of Roswell, Georgia, where we all lived. We had black-and-white pictures made with the band name on the pictures and attached a song list to the back. It made a nice little package for our PR marketing. We played at all the popular places that bands played on Roswell Road in Atlanta and we traveled and played in different cities too. It was really fun and very rewarding. After playing together for a couple of years, Randall and I fell in love and got married in 1977.

Our band continued to play around town for several years, until we had our first child, a boy, we named him Mitchell. Then two-and-a-half years later we had a little girl, Jessica. We had daytime jobs but we kept the band going as best we could. We really wanted children and our first years with them were wonderful, happy and fun. We had a bass boat and went camping and fishing as often as we could with them. We even took our dog, Jolly, camping with us. It was exactly what I had dreamed about as a little girl. We were very happy.

When our son was three years old and our daughter was one, we wanted to leave apartment living and found a rental home in East Cobb County. It was in a cul-de-sac in a nice neighborhood with good schools. It had three bedrooms and a bonus room in the basement. Our drummer needed a place to live so we rented the bonus room to him.

Just before we moved in, the interior of the home had been painted and the trim, including on the windows, had been stained. Early one weekday morning, two weeks after we moved in, and after my husband had left for work, I decided to jump in the shower before the kids were up. About 10 minutes into my shower, my toddler opened the bathroom door, came inside, pulled back the shower curtain and said, "Mommy, the couch is on fire." At that moment I noticed a cloud of black, sooty smoke rolling into the bathroom then into the shower up at the ceiling. I was caught off guard—he had been in bed when I got into the shower.

I turned the shower off, grabbed a towel and threw it over my shoulder, got out quickly, grabbed his hand, and said, "What do you mean the couch is on fire?" He did his best to explain it to me, but he was a scared three-year-old. Once I walked into our bedroom and saw that the thick black smoke was already filling the room, I knew we were in big trouble. The house was a ranch style. The family room, with the front door, and the kitchen were in the middle of the house. The den was on one end of the house and the bedrooms were at the opposite end of the house.

Suddenly, the smoke was so thick we couldn't see or

breathe. I knew the couch my son was talking about was on fire in the den at the other end of the house. The den had a rich, wood paneling which I'm sure ignited very easily and explained why this happened so quickly. Also in that den were my piano, which my grandparents had given me, my black acoustic Ovation guitar, and Randall's Gibson electric 335 guitar.

I told my son to get down on the floor of the hallway and I got down there with him on our hands and knees. We then crawled to my daughter's bedroom. I opened the door and saw her quietly standing up in her crib—then the black, sooty smoke completely filled her room and I could no longer see her or see my hand in front of my face. I knew then we would not make it to the front door and would have to go out her bedroom window.

We got to the window and, because it was newly stained, it was stuck and wouldn't open. I kept pushing on it and with, I guess, the help of my adrenaline, I was able to get the window up. Once it opened, it sucked out all the black smoke in the bedroom which began to roll out the window in huge gusts. For the brief moment before the smoke started rolling out, I was able to see two fire trucks already in front of the house, neighbors walking towards us, and a black cloud of smoke over the house.

I suddenly realized I'm going out this window with my children, but I'm butt naked and don't really care. I lifted my son up to the window and told him I have to drop him down to the ground and he's just going to have to do his best to fall. I'm moving very quickly because the severity of the situation is finally hitting me. It's only been a matter of minutes since he opened the bathroom door, and I'm just doing automatic actions to try to save us without really processing how or why it happened.

After dropping my son out the window (it's about a six-foot drop), I started groping around the crib to find my daughter. I dangled her out of the window and told my son to try to catch her. He did. Next I propelled myself out that window headfirst, landing next to the kids. I picked up my crying daughter, who was unharmed. Then I hold and comfort her and my son in front of my naked body, trying to hide a little from all the neighbors who are now running across the front yard towards us. Suddenly, our drummer, who's living in our basement bedroom, came out from the sliding glass door in the bonus room after being awakened by the glass breaking in the upstairs windows and the smell of smoke. Although disoriented, he saw us standing behind the bushes in front of the house. He ran back into the house to bring me a blanket.

Miraculously, none of us were hurt in any way.

Soon a neighbor brought me a robe, then another neighbor took the kids to her home to care for them. I stood in front of the house and watched a fireman chop down the front door with an axe while another fireman was chopping a hole in the roof over the den. Suddenly, a blaze of fire came out of that hole. I was in total shock and couldn't believe what has happened in a short period. Someone asked me if they can call my husband, and I barely remembered his boss's phone number. Then someone else came over and asked if I would like to come home with her and take a shower. My response was, "No, thank you, I just had one." She looked at me as if

I'm crazy and she didn't know what to say. A few hours later I went to her bathroom, looked in the mirror and saw that I was covered head to toe with black soot from the smoke. It must have clung to me because I was wet from my shower. I didn't remember my kids being covered in soot and certainly didn't realize the fact that it was all over me. In hindsight, I can only attribute that to being in shock.

Before too long, my husband came home, just in time to watch the firemen drag all of our water-soaked and ruined furniture outside onto a huge pile of junk. Anything that wasn't ruined by water or fire was ruined by smoke and heat. Our toothbrushes had melted to the hardware in the bathrooms, and our clothes and mattresses smelled like smoke.

The fire investigators came that day. We figured out that as soon as I had gotten into the shower, my son got up and found a lighter and started playing with it on the couch in the den (without letting me know he was up). Mitchell told us he was holding a pillow over the flame, which caught it on fire. He explained how he tried to hit the pillow on the couch to put it out, which made it worse. He then watched the couch go up in flames, which immediately lit up the wall paneling. Fearing he would get in trouble, he was scared to tell me until it was pretty far-gone.

He was always a very independent child. He liked to wander away from me in large department stores and at strip malls. He never seemed to worry about losing me and he didn't fear getting lost because he always knew where he was. All I had to do was find the toy department or toy store—he would be there having a blast playing with the toys. He was without a doubt a very challenging child, but I loved him dearly then, as I do now.

Thank goodness he came inside the shower to tell me about the fire. I shudder to think what would have happened if he had waited longer than he did. We were out of that house within minutes of him alerting me. Even though we lost everything, I never really mourned the loss of our stuff because I was so grateful that we all survived...it was just that close.

We moved into my father's house. Thank goodness he had a new home in Kennesaw with two empty bedrooms. About the same time that we had married, Dad found the love of his life. She was only six years older than I was but she just adored him. They married and she would be his partner for the rest of his life. She and Dad took such good care of each other. She is a sweet person and has been very loving to my sisters and me. We were ecstatic to see Dad happy and in high spirits and we all got along well with her. She has been a wonderful stepmother, grandmother to my kids and grandkids and to my sisters' kids, and I'm very grateful she's in my life.

They had been married about three years when the fire occurred and they invited us to live with them while the house was being repaired. He even let the drummer sleep on his couch in the family room. After our house was repaired, which took about four months, we moved back into it. This created an awkward situation with our son because we had to scold him for playing with the lighter, but we had to be careful to do it with love because he'd seen the damage he'd caused and knew he was to blame. I have wondered my whole life how much that fire affected him emotionally.

CHAPTER 6

A Time of Constant Crisis

When my son reached the age to start going to school, I read a newspaper article about a woman in our county who wanted to start a hotline for victims of domestic violence. The article was announcing training for volunteers, with a phone number to call for anyone interested in volunteering to work on the hotline.

When I finished reading the article, my mind was flooded with memories of how it felt back in college when I was abused and I realized how lucky I was to get out quickly before I was badly hurt. It crossed my mind that for so many women who were married with kids and dependent on their abuser, it would not be that easy for them. I thought that, having experienced violence myself, I might be able to connect with other victims of domestic violence. I felt a strong desire to get involved with the hotline and attended the training. I was really committed to that cause and it led to me working in the domestic violence movement for the next six-plus years.

The hotline was such a success that it eventually led to the organization raising enough money to open the first shelter for abused women and children in Cherokee County. I became the first shelter director. I also helped start the first battered women's shelter in Forsyth County and became their first executive director. In 1987, after lots of training on the laws as set out in Georgia's Family Violence Act, I asked the circuit court judge to appoint me as the circuit's first legal advocate for woman who needed to obtain a Temporary Protective Order (TPO) under the Family Violence Act without an attorney.

He did.

I was then allowed to assist women in filling out petitions for TPOs and to appear with them in court as an advocate. It was a fantastic job for me at the time and I was excited to help so many women obtain orders of protection at no cost to them. I also trained volunteers and helped facilitate the in-house support groups. Additionally, I worked at the state level to improve laws for victims of violence by lobbying members of the House and Senate to pass better laws. It was a group effort by formerly battered women and members of the state coalition of shelters that ultimately led to the creation of a task force, chaired by a woman representative in the legislature, to address how our state could better serve victims of violence.

This was very rewarding work. However, after I'd spent every day for several years doing crisis intervention at work, problems with my son were escalating and it felt as if I had to do crisis intervention at home as well.

Mitchell was starting to have behavioral problems. In the third grade, he was tested by the school and found to have ADD (attention deficit disorder). His teachers wanted me to put him on the drug Ritalin (very commonly prescribed then as now) but I decided against it, fearing too many kids were being put on that drug without our having a full understanding of the side effects. By the sixth grade he was having a great deal of problems paying attention and completing and turning in his schoolwork. By the seventh grade, he was getting suspended from school. He was also sneaking out of our house to meet up with kids from school and he was getting into legal trouble.

My husband and I were really challenged by how to address his behavioral problems and we tried various disciplines and ways to respond. We often did not agree on what was causing the problem or how to handle his punishment, which created stress in our relationship. It reached a point where I thought we needed professional intervention, but my husband took a more relaxed attitude, insisting our son was just "being a boy" and would grow out of it, as he and his brothers had.

When my son was around eleven years old, I'd hired a babysitter for the kids for the couple of hours they were home after school before I got home from work. The girl was a senior in high school and had come recommended to me by a friend. It didn't last very long because I soon started getting notices from my bank that checks written out of a closed-account checkbook were being cashed—and then returned to the grocery stores that had cashed them, because the account was closed. Apparently, the babysitter had been stealing checks out of old checkbook boxes she found in my basement. She'd take them to grocery stores that didn't ask to see her ID and she'd cash them by forging my name. I called the police, and that's when the kids told me about what else she had been doing with them. She had been smoking pot in front of them and letting them smoke it with her. I was livid and reported to the police every bit of information I had about her and her family. I told the police that I knew where she lived and kept calling to reach her mother or anyone but no one answered. It looked as if they had completely disappeared. Before calling the police, I'd gone to her house several times when I couldn't get an answer. It appeared to be empty so I assumed she figured things were about to hit the fan and it would be easy to nail her for the stolen checks, so she vanished.

Next we began to suspect our 11 year old son was smoking pot on a regular basis. After the babysitter incident, the drug abuse and acting out got worse. Mitchell was jumping out of his bedroom window from the second floor during the night and sneaking back in through the front door. As embarrassing as it is to say, we apparently didn't catch on to his outside activity for a while. Once we realized what he was doing, we drove around looking for him, which was a total waste of time. At the time, we lived close to Lake Allatoona and there were so many woods around us, it was impossible to find him in the dark. Plus, we were sure he was with other kids from school. We sat up several nights waiting for his return and when we'd catch him, we'd ground him, take privileges away, or both. He never respected any grounding or house rules, nor cared what his consequences were.

When no punishment worked, we called the police several times. They told us to file an unruly petition on him.

An unruly petition is about the only recourse that a parent in Georgia had when a juvenile refuses to obey or abide by their rules. The court then has authority to use resources available to them in hopes it will help to change the unruly behavior. We filed several petitions, but it had little effect on Mitchell's behavior. He eventually was arrested for arson and served time in the Youth Detention Center (YDC). The juvenile judges (yes, several separate cases) sentenced him to attend or participate in any and all programs available to the court to try to rehabilitate him, but the situation just got worse. When he was twelve, they sent him to a rehab center in Augusta, Georgia, called Alchemy.

He escaped.

They sent him to a locked-down residential center in Marietta.

He escaped again.

After that they just held him in YDC until his sentence was up and he returned home.

It was a very stressful situation. We were desperate to figure out something we could do to stop his destructive behavior, but we were not able to find anything that worked. We tried rewards and punishments to no avail. At one point, when he was still twelve, he spent a few days in the regional mental health hospital where he was diagnosed with depression. I really didn't think that was accurate but I had no clue what was happening in that head of his. Eventually, the County Board of Education referred him to an alternative school and he began attending it. That started in the seventh grade. He didn't graduate high school but he did get his GED not long after he would have graduated.

We hoped that something would help. Nothing did. The stress on our family was immeasurable. We were not equipped with the knowledge or experience on how to respond to his repeated acting out and obvious need for help. The most damage was done to our marriage because with each incident that occurred we could not agree on how to handle him. Things were getting worse and then our daughter told us of an event that would bring us all to the depths of despair.

She was about nine years old when she told us that her brother had done something extremely disturbing and traumatic to her. My husband and I weren't present when it occurred, but we eventually became aware of it. It was serious enough that we enlisted professional intervention by various people trained to respond in crisis situation. My husband and I did not know how to handle the situation but did the best we could at the time. I am so sorry we couldn't protect them.

I'm not going to share the details here because it's their story and not my place to tell what happened, except to say it really hurt our kids, especially my daughter, and it ripped our family apart and had long lasting effects on all of our lives

I have spent most of my adult life trying to make up for the things I did wrong where my kids are concerned, but you can only change the present. I think I've bent over backwards trying to help them by being there for them and loving them as adults, but it has been very challenging. My daughter became very dependent on me and I probably enabled some of that behavior by not encouraging her to stand on her own two feet. It's still an ongoing struggle and I will continue to accept my part for failing as a parent when they were children.

A year after the traumatic event occurred between my kids, and my husband and I were trying to help our family recover as best we could, although the damage done to our marriage and our relationship was irreparable. We were blaming each other and we were dealing with our pain and guilt in different ways. The ordeal had driven us apart instead of bringing us closer together. The marriage was over, but we didn't split yet. My husband had some personal problems spiraling out of control that I was not happy about and wanted nothing to do with. I was drinking heavily to cope with the constant pressure of being in crisis mode at all times...at work and at home. It was hard to get through each day. I started drinking when I got home from work, drank while cooking dinner, and drank while eating dinner, each night. It was mostly wine, at the beginning. I thought it was the solution to my problems. I was still functioning and making it to work every day but I started staying at work later and later to avoid going home. Using work and wine, I tried to escape my problems. I didn't know what else to do.

Eventually, my drinking took a toll on me and my job, which led to my being fired. It was taking a toll on the kids too. I didn't see that at the time.

I decided that, anyway, I needed to find a job that paid more than working for a nonprofit did, which back then was next to nothing. Right after I lost my job, our grandmother, our mom's stepmother, had gifted my sisters and me some blue chip stock certificates. We weren't really close to her and I think it was mainly a way for her to get a tax write-off. We did appreciate it and it was perfect timing. My sister Christy and I decided to use the money to go back to school and try to get good-paying jobs. We decided on going to paralegal school. I had been helping women get protective orders in court for years and I thought I was really good at legal stuff, so I had an interest in staying in the legal field.

We applied and were accepted to an ABA-approved paralegal school in Buckhead, a community in Atlanta. We went full-time for about nine months, then we graduated in 1992, receiving our certificates with a specialty in civil litigation. It was one of the hardest things I have ever done and I'm sure Christy thought so too.

But it was the beginning of being able to start over. I knew I would now be able to find work that paid well so I could leave my husband. Even though I felt a deep sense of accomplishment, I was overwhelmed, scared and confused and looking for a way out. Once again, I didn't handle it well. I made mistakes. I hurt my husband and my children and I regret how it all ended. I wish I had been more cognizant of the repercussions that would affect our family for the rest of our lives. There were no coaches for this kind of stuff back then. At least, I didn't know about them. It was just one more of many difficult times I would face in my life journey, but not the last mistake I would make along the way.

CHAPTER 7

"Do you know where your daughter is?"

Before my marriage ended, I reconnected with my old singing partner from my college years, the percussionist who also played guitar and sang. We started playing and singing in coffeehouses again. He was divorced, and I needed to escape the pressure of everything that was going wrong in my life, my family and my marriage. My husband, Randall, had continued to play music, write songs and have a band, but his music style, mostly the blues, was not the style of singing that came naturally to me, though I enjoyed listening to music in that genre.

I missed singing the songs my old singing partner and I had sung during college, with me harmonizing. When we starting playing together again, it was the first time I had felt real happiness and joy in years. It wasn't long after we started playing together that I filed for divorce.

I knew singing was something I could do well and do right. When we got back together, we sounded as great as we had sixteen years before. I was able to get a little bit of relief from the pain and sorrow I'd felt over the past four years. I had also just started working for an attorney as his secretary/paralegal. It was a small office and the job didn't pay that much, but it was a start and gave me some experience in a legal environment.

When our divorce was final, the kids were thirteen and eleven. The situation was rocky, to say the least. My husband would have physical custody of our son and I would have physical custody of our daughter. They were both devastated; I think we all were. I honestly did not know what to do next, except to sing and to carry on with the next chapter in my life. There's no doubt I was on the rebound from the demise of my marriage.

My singing partner and I had become intimate, and he had been a shoulder to cry on and a good and understanding friend. Sometime after my divorce was filed, we started living together with my daughter. We continued singing, and I was working for a different attorney strictly as a paralegal. At almost age forty, my partner wanted to go back to school to get his degree in music. He did that, but he liked school so much that he remained a student for several more years after getting his bachelor's degree in music composition, working towards a master's degree. He had a son from his previous marriage who lived with his ex-wife. His child support payments were minimal but I wasn't making enough money to support us all. He was perfectly happy living off student loans—I was not.

Both of my children were struggling at the time, which affected their school work. I thought I loved him as a partner, but I was looking for someone to save me from all the dysfunction. Unfortunately, I didn't see that at the time and we got married in December of 1994. I hoped getting married might stabilize our life, but having a stepfather only made the kids more resentful and his attempts at discipline didn't work any better than mine.

My daughter was angry with me for everything and anything, and she demanded to live with her father, which I refused to allow. By that time, I had heard that my son had been smoking pot with his father and that they were selling it.

I felt my daughter began to rebel when I refused to allow her to move in with her father. She started sneaking out of her bedroom window at night and disappearing. She flat out told me she would continue to act out and cause me stress until I let her move in with her father. She meant it, too. I was drinking more to escape the pain and, as usual, not handling the situation well, but I knew I could not let her control the house. The only problem was I wasn't controlling it either. I was not equipped with the answers for this situation even after all the practice with her brother. I admit I did not know what to do.

Then one night when she was fourteen years old and had a girlfriend staying over, they decided it would be a good idea to steal my car in the middle of the night. They wanted to meet some boys from my daughter's childhood neighborhood, which was about twenty-five miles away. Neither knew how to drive, much less drive a stick shift, but they were resourceful and determined. They got out the car manual and found the instructions on how to change the gears. Somehow they got the car started (after taking the keys out of my purse), pulled out of our apartment parking lot and got onto the interstate. They thought they knew how to get back to our old neighborhood but failed to take the right turn off the interstate and got lost in the Bankhead Highway area, a very bad part of town known to Atlanta drug users as "the Bluff."

A patrol car spotted these two young girls when the car stalled at a red light. The police pulled them over. They knew the girls were in the wrong place at the wrong time with no licenses and decided to have mercy on them. One of the officers called and woke me up about 3:30 a.m. and asked if I had a daughter, giving me her name. I replied yes. Then I was trying to wake up quickly and get my wits about me, and he asked, "Do you know where your daughter is?" Fearing his response, I replied, "Uh, asleep in her bed?" I knew at that point it was wishful thinking, but they had been in bed when I fell asleep—I had checked on them. The officer then said he regretted to inform me that she and her friend had apparently stolen my car, gotten lost in "the Bluffs," and had rolled through a red light when he spotted them. He said that because they were only fourteen, they would give me one hour to come get them and pick up my car before they would have it impounded.

Well, she had taken my only car and my husband did not have a car at that point. So I called her dad, who helped me get her home—and my car, so I'd be able to go to work the next morning. Not long after this incident, I let her move to her dad's house just to see if it helped one or both of us.

This would not be the only time my car was stolen in the middle of the night by my kids, it happened so many times we had to start writing down the mileage and/or hiding the keys. Like many teenagers, they were really good at being sneaky. I also thought it might be karma since I had snuck out with the car once when I was in high school too.

In the meantime, my son was continuing to do things that got him locked up in YDC and to use drugs. He eventually became banned from living in the county where he lived with his father, so we decided upon his release that he would live with us because we lived in another county. We made him sign a contract, in which we laid out the house rules. He agreed to abide by our terms. The judge released him but gave him probation and put him on house arrest to serve the remaining time on probation. He had to wear a monitored ankle bracelet; and he had to stay within a five-mile radius of the house. I welcomed the device, thinking it would be a great deterrent.

Then he decided he was going to be a skinhead and began looking the part, shaving his head bald, wearing suspenders, and sporting army boots with red laces. By then he had many friends who were also skinheads, and he was acting like he was some kind of white supremacist at the age of sixteen. He was listening to "Oi!" music and "ska" music. I'm not knowledgeable enough to explain what that is because I couldn't listen to it.

I have only a guess about where his mind-set originated. His father and I were liberal minded and it never crossed our minds that our kids would be attracted to a racist or hateful kind of lifestyle. I guess it was the furthest thing he could find from what his parents believed in. I also think he was looking to fit in somewhere. He seemed to think this group of kids would protect him and have his back.

I knew he needed help, but at that point, he was belligerent and rebellious and wasn't going to cooperate or listen to anything I had to say, much less to address his own problems.

As far as he was concerned, he didn't need or want help.

Thankfully, someone who turned out to be a great friend made a suggestion to me. I listened to it and took her advice.

It would eventually help to change everything.

CHAPTER 8

"If you want what we have…"

One day a girl friend of mine told me about a rehab program for young people that her son had gotten involved in. It was called Atlanta Insight. Her son and my son were the same age. They had met in school and were friends and had gotten in some trouble together. I told her I was living in "parent hell" for years and didn't know what to do next. She told me the rehab program had a bunch of other young kids who were all having drug and life problems. Being with other kids with the same issues and having a young drug counselor leading the group seemed to have a positive effect on her son. She also told me that the parents of these kids had their own meeting that went on at the same time as the kids' meeting, which was twice a week.

She said the parents that attended these meetings had the same problems I did and shared their struggles with each other. She also said there were solutions to our problems and that, if I reached out for help, I might find it. She also said she and her husband found the meetings to be a really good support system for them. She invited me several times and at first I said thanks, but no thanks. She continued to encourage me to go and to take my son. She kept telling me I had nothing to lose and might possibly find something that would help. She was right. Nothing I was doing worked and my life had become very depressing. I was desperate, sad and distraught, so I agreed to go and told my son he was going with me.

The meetings were free and at a church really close to where we lived. They were open to kids in a certain age range who had drug problems. We pulled up to the church and into the parking lot where he saw about twenty-five kids his age hanging out. We'd gotten there a little early. He got out of the car and walked over to where a group of kids were standing. He had a bald head and was wearing his boots and suspenders. When he reached the group, they all quickly surrounded him and asked his name. Some of them even hugged him. I was immediately relieved for myself and he looked relieved too, which allowed me to focus on where I needed to be.

So I went into the church. It seemed like there were about a hundred more teenagers, some were running around and some were setting up chairs in a circle. Someone asked if I needed help finding the parents meeting, then she took me there. Inside the room were adults, mostly my age, who were also setting up chairs in a circle. When they saw me, many stopped what they were doing and introduced themselves. They asked my name and welcomed me and told me to sit anywhere. The circle of chairs looked like there were about fifty places for people to sit and I was thinking that the whole thing was way bigger than I had anticipated.

People were starting to trickle in and sit down and sure enough by the time the meeting started, there must have been fifty or more parents in the room. The first thing I noticed was the looks on their faces. They were smiling and greeting each other with hugs, some were even laughing. The first thing that crossed my mind was that if these people were living in parent hell like I was, how were they laughing?

The meeting started. One of the parents was facilitating and leading the meeting. He opened the meeting by saying his name, then he sent around a paper containing the twelve steps of Alcoholics Anonymous (AA) and each person read a step and passed it on to the next person until all the steps had been read. Then he read a paragraph found in the Big Book of AA.

I can't say I remember much of anything else said in that meeting—with one exception. I remember hearing someone read this sentence, "If you have decided you want what we have and are willing to go to any lengths to get it— then you are ready to take certain steps." During that next hour, I heard people share stories about their parent hell, but they were happy. They all seemed genuinely happy. So I thought either they were pretending, or my story was just worse than theirs. One thing I knew for sure when I left: I was impressed. If they really were happy then I wanted what they had and I was willing to go to any lengths to get it. It's a good thing I didn't know then what lengths I would have to go to, but suffice it to say I knew at that point I was at the right place. My friend who'd invited me was there and she told me that if I liked what I heard, then I should come back to the next meeting. She said the meetings were free and she hoped I would keep coming back. For the first time in years,

I found a tiny bit of hope and decided I would try it, but what about my son? I was wondering what he thought about his meeting. I immediately started to focus all my thoughts on him.

When I saw him after his meeting, he told me he loved it and that the kids were going somewhere for coffee and they wanted him to go. One of the kids came up to me and told me how glad they all were that he had come. I told her he was on house arrest and his curfew was 10:00 p.m. and she promised he would be home by then.

I was overwhelmed and wasn't sure it was all for real. The girl said the counselors always went to coffee with them and he would be safe and I could talk to them if I was worried. So I did, then I let him go for coffee. He was home on time and said he wanted to go to the next meeting, so we started going to these meetings together and things got better, a lot better. My husband even went with me to some of the meetings.

When I saw how our life was improving, I started thinking it might be good for my daughter to get involved. Even though she was still living with her dad, we had visitation time, and soon she tried it out and seemed to like it. Eventually, things got better between us and she even moved back in with us. The counselors recommended both kids go to an outpatient program, which they did. In the long run, I spent thousands of dollars for their participation in outpatient treatment hoping it would make them want to change their way of life. The kids in outpatient hung out together all the time, and they didn't use drugs or drink. That reduced my stress and it gave me the emotional break I needed so I could recover too.

The parents in my group were working the twelve steps of Al-Anon. The steps are slightly modified for the people dealing with the alcoholic. So, I got a sponsor, and I eventually sponsored the newcomer parents. I started to believe it was possible that my family could recover and that I could move past the nightmare I had been living. I joined this group of parents in 1996. I have to say that without them and without learning some tools from the twelve steps of Al-Anon, I never would have made it through parent hell. Some of their stories were worse than mine and it took me a while to really find my faith, surrender, and turn my will over to a power greater than myself. I remember sharing in one meeting that I just couldn't be happy until my kids were happy. Then someone asked me, "What happens if your kids never get happy?" That hit me like a ton of bricks. It had never crossed my mind that they might never be happy.

I continued to attend the parent group for many years, even after my kids left that program. I will be forever grateful to the members of that parent group who really saved my life. It was during that time that I realized I was an alcoholic and that I couldn't expect my kids to get or be sober if I couldn't find my own sobriety. So I began attending AA. Though I have had a couple of short slips since 1996, my life has been forever changed and I've survived numerous traumas without the need to have a drink. To this day, I remain friends with the majority of those parents from the rehab group. Many of their kids have gone on to lead happy and productive lives, get married and have their own children.

Most of us celebrate the wonder, excitement and joy of being made grandparents. It's such an amazing and precious gift.

To all of those parents who attended meetings and shared their experience, strength and hope with me, all I can say is "Thank you for sharing your hardships" and "I still love you guys."

Unfortunately, my own kids did not find sobriety. But I learned how to let go and let God take care of the problems. It sounds harsh, but I felt as though I had focused so much attention on their happiness, their recovery, their needs and their problems that I had ignored my own. I knew that needed to change. I had to learn how to love unconditionally but not accept their bad behavior. I know as parents we feel we are supposed to put their needs first at all times. But when you're flying on a plane and the oxygen masks drop down, you're told to put your mask on first and then on the child.

If you are experiencing a similar type of parent hell please find an Al-Anon or other similar support group. You probably won't like the first meeting, but if the people attending seem happy, then give it another chance and keep going back. I thought at first that the parents in my group, who all seemed enormously happy, were faking. Once I realized it was real, I still didn't like what they wanted me to do, but I kept going back and finally I had a real smile, too. Those tools have stuck with me through every catastrophe and hard life experience. Remember that happiness is an "inside job"—you have to work on you. I thank God and the universe for helping me continue to rely on the God within that keeps me smiling.

CHAPTER 9

Parent Hell and Drug Addiction

My husband and I took different paths. We sang together at several Atlanta Insight events with the kids and parents over the next few years, but he planned to remain a college student until he received his doctorate and I was on a quest to heal from the trauma of my past. My husband even wrote and musical play called "Come Fly With Me" that was loosely based on a young people's drug rehab program and recovery. He wrote it to obtain credit as a music composition major at the university he attended. It was performed several times at the Rialto Theatre in downtown Atlanta and many of the kids and parents in the program, including myself, sang and participated in the musical. It was really fun.

Unfortunately, being married to someone who planned on being a perpetual student was not part of my path or plan. As it turned out, we were much better friends and singing partners than we were marriage partners. So I moved out, taking my daughter with me. By this time, I was working for a bigger company and earning a good income, able to make it on my own.

A few months after leaving my husband, we reconciled and he moved in with me and my daughter. We decided we wanted to add a dog to the family. I've always loved dogs, particularly Australian shepherds, aka aussies, so we found a local breeder and went and picked out a puppy. My intention was to bring home one puppy. But while the three of us were there, we fell in love with three puppies. The breeder had two separate litters from two female dogs for us to choose from. She also had a beagle puppy. I became partial to one of the red merle little girls, and my daughter became partial to a boy from the different litter. We played with all the puppies for over an hour paying attention to their personalities. While I wasn't paying much attention, my husband was bonding with beagle puppy!! I was not prepared to take home three puppies, but the woman told us I could bring any of them back for a refund if it didn't work out. So we took them home and named the little girl Lisa and the fluffy little boy we named Levi. The beagle we named Rusty. They quickly and easily became part of the family and we loved and enjoyed them for many years to come. Sadly, Rusty was hit by a car about a year after we got him.

By this time, my son had decided to join the army. He went to boot camp, but while training, he was dishonorably discharged when a picture surfaced of him either wearing or holding the robes of the KKK. This apparent association with the KKK was clearly the influence of my mother's boyfriend at the time—he had connections to the KKK and collected Nazi memorabilia. My son had lived with them for a short period just before leaving for boot camp. After being sent home from boot camp, he would be in and out of jail frequently in the years that followed. He was on a path towards a major drug addiction and although it was very sad for me to watch him make such bad choices, I was no longer responsible for him and had my hands full with my daughter.

My daughter ended up pregnant at age sixteen. Her baby boy was born out of wedlock when she was seventeen years old. Though she tried very hard to be a good mother, she was not ready and neither was the father; no one really is at seventeen. She didn't graduate from high school but I was proud of her determination when she successfully got her GED.

Her boy was born in November 1999 and he was, and is, greatly loved by all of us. Our dog Levi was his greatest protector. Levi followed him around everywhere and lay by his side any time he was playing on the floor.

Jessica and the baby's father tried to be parents together. I let them live with me, thinking it would help them. After three months of them trying to be a family and months of constant fighting, it just wasn't working. He moved out, leaving her alone to care for the baby. Although I helped her care for Brody, I felt that being a single mother took its toll on Jessica.

In fact, after the father left she started using hard drugs. It got to the point that I was starting to be the main caretaker of my grandson because she was staying out all night and not coming home in the morning. I knew she loved that baby, she was just young, she was scared and she had no other coping skills to deal with stress.

Don't get me wrong. I loved and adored my grandson, Brody, and he has been such a wonderful blessing in my life.

But it left me in a predicament because I couldn't go to work in the mornings when she wasn't there. Even though Jessica was working at a day care center, I couldn't enroll him in day care because I did not have the parental authority. Jessica's addiction got worse, and she lost custody of her son when she couldn't pass a drug test at a DFACS court hearing. I was granted custody for two years when he was eighteen months old. I'd loved him before that, but soon came to love that little boy as though he were my own.

Those next couple of years were tough on me. Even though I had now enrolled him in day care, I was basically alone paying for it, at more than $800 a month. That was a huge chunk out of my salary. And I was living in a large home. We'd moved into it after the baby was born because I thought a family of three would be living there with us and that they would help pay rent. At least that was the original plan. When that didn't work out, both of my parents were very helpful and supportive. My father and stepmom contributed to the monthly day care expenses and it helped me a lot. Except for the financial stress, the first years with my grandson were very happy and we bonded together.

During this period, my husband was living with us but surviving on student loans and unable to contribute financially to our household. When it started to feel like I was supporting all three of us alone, I became extremely frustrated and asked him to move out. We really didn't have much of a relationship at this point, we were both on separate paths going in different directions.

My daughter lived there off and on. She desperately wanted to have a skill that could help her get a good job so she enrolled in a technical school using student loans and she did pretty well for a time. She seemed to really want to be clean and happy, and she started being a responsible mother.

But it was short-lived.

My hopes were dashed again after she admitted she was maintaining her addiction on a daily basis with small amounts of heroin. That's when I told her she had to find a treatment program and stay in it until she got her shit together. I told her that until she was completely sober, she could not live in my house again.

She did find a treatment center and was admitted. She stayed for three, maybe four, weeks then got mad and left. She expected me to save her again. But I said no way, you cannot come back until you get sober.

She had become dependent on me emotionally and financially. It felt like constant chaos and drama in our home and we rarely had a moment's peace. Somehow I had become part of the problem and found it difficult to see the solution and now there was an innocent child in the mix and I had to focus my attention on him.

Still, I tried to have a normal life. I played my guitar, and I was singing and playing with friends from my parent group. I starting dating someone in the program, but it felt as though I couldn't go anywhere or do anything without Jessica creating a crisis. I believe it was around this time that her mental problems surfaced. Around age eighteen, she was exhibiting signs of irrational paranoia. She was constantly thinking and imagining that horrible accidents would happen, causing her to live in fear of the future. It appeared to me at the time she just refused to be happy. In hindsight, I know being happy was not a choice for her. Her illness was in control of her actions.

Unfortunately, I did not really understand what was happening. I thought if I just helped her to improve her situation, she wouldn't feel so hopeless. So, I helped her get a car so she could get around but she got several tickets, for which she didn't pay or didn't show up to court. Eventually she was pulled over and arrested for driving with a suspended license and taken to jail. I left her there. She got out on her own bond, but I refused to get her car out of the tow lot, so she lost it.

There was constant stress on me and it wasn't long before the stress took its toll. One night I went out and bought a small bottle of wine, came home, and drank it. I hadn't had a drinkin six years and I knew it wasn't the solution, but it was almost as if I wanted to show the wine I could handle it. The next morning I woke up and didn't want to be sober. That scared me not just because I didn't have any friends that drank—all my friends were sober—but I knew that wasn't what I wanted for my life. I never liked going to bars so I just went to a meeting that night, picked up a white chip (a white chip signifies a person's desire to stop drinking for a day), and then went every night after that until I wanted to be sober and became engulfed in my sobriety.

Part of doing that meant I had to let go of a lot of things. The rent on my house was draining me financially so I had to get out of it quickly. I asked the father of my grandson if he would take physical custody of Brody for a few months while I got my act together. He agreed. It was the hardest thing I've ever done, and it broke my heart and brought me to tears frequently. I spent every weekend and holiday with my grandson, but I knew I had to make some major changes quickly.

I told my daughter I was moving out of that house at the end of the current month with both of the dogs and that she wasn't coming with me. She started attending AA, found a job and rented a room from a woman close to where I was going. Jessica started to get serious about her sobriety and started living clean. Soon she met someone in the program and they started dating. Their relationship lasted a long time, and so did her sobriety.

The person I was dating, who I mentioned earlier, along with a few other friends, helped me move out and settle into a one-bedroom flat at half the rent of the house. I had to leave a ton of stuff in that house because I had nowhere to put it.

Then, against some people's advice, my boyfriend, James, moved into the flat with me and soon we fell madly in love.

CHAPTER 10

They Say Third Time's a Charm

I'm sure you won't be surprised when I tell you that I thought this was the real and final "one." Neither of us were looking for love but after living together for six months we got engaged. We seemed like perfect partners. I was forty-seven; he was six months younger and very handsome (to me). We came from the same upbringing in the same community and had gone to the same high school. I'd known his brother in high school, but I hadn't really known him. We promised we would grow old together. I was done with relationship drama and so was he. He had been divorced for twelve years and had two sons from that marriage. They were almost adults. He was also a musician, a harmonica player. He played harmonica with a band of guys about twenty years younger, and he could play a little guitar though he didn't play it in the band.

We had the most wonderful wedding. It was at his family's lake house. All of our family and friends were there, including my friends from the parent group, my sisters, my mother and her partner, and my father and his wife. He gave me away (again). I sang to my husband after the ceremony, in front of all the guests. It was magical.

At the reception, James's band played and there were fireworks at the end, reflecting on the lake. It was a dream come true and to this day it's one of the best memories of my life.

I really loved his brother and his brother's wife, his sister, and his parents, too, who were all really sweet to me. My dad and his dad got along great and seemed to have a lot in common. To all eyes it appeared a perfect match and I was ecstatically happy.

While we were on our honeymoon, my daughter called me. She said Brody's father called her and said she needed to come get her son, that he was "done." She was living with her boyfriend at the time, and he didn't want her son living with them.

Jessica and I had spent a lot of time with Brody, even while he was living with his father. Brody, then three years old, was the ring bearer in our wedding. He was happy when he was with us but not happy when it was time to go home with his father. He had been with his mom during the week we were preparing for the wedding day, and he'd had so much fun at the wedding all dressed up in his little tuxedo and playing with all the kids.

It may be that when he got back to his father's house after the wedding, he spent most of the time telling him that he wanted to "go home." I'm not sure what happened; I just know we weren't about to make him stay someplace he wasn't happy. James and I discussed it. It was his idea to tell my daughter to get Brody, take him to our apartment, and stay there while we were on our honeymoon. We would figure it out when we got back.

After we discussed the situation, James said we could probably live in his parent's house because they lived in Florida full-time and kept a house just for their trips back to Atlanta. He asked his parents if it was okay for us to stay there until we could find a house. They were fine with that. So Jessica and Brody lived in our one-bedroom flat with both the dogs until we bought a house, which was about four months later. Then while James and I moved into our first home with our dogs, Jessica and Brody moved into an apartment. She was able to rent because she had been working long enough to qualify. Brody was very happy to be with her and we were hopeful she would stay stable. They rode the bus for an hour every day to her work at a day care center and back home every day for almost nine months. Her apartment was in a rough part of town and far away from us, so eventually I helped her rent an apartment closer to where we were living. It was a really good time, and everyone was happy, but it didn't last. Brody was five years old when Jessica lost the day care job and started using again.

One afternoon I got a call from my daughter. She had overdosed on heroin and was in the emergency room at the hospital. Brody was at his day care center and the ER nurse told her they weren't going to release her any time soon. My daughter had told the staff that she had to get her son at his day care. They apparently called DFACS and told them what was happening and that they weren't releasing her to pick up her son. She asked me to get him before DFACS got there. I knew this meant that if my husband and I picked him up from day care, he would be staying with us for a long time. So I talked to James and, thankfully, he agreed he didn't want Brody in foster care. He went to the day care, where we had picked him up many times before, and brought him to our home.

I contacted DFACS and told them we had picked him up. The caseworker informed me that we needed to get legal custody of him because he could not go back to his mother's custody. We did what they told us to do and he lived with us from age five until he was almost nine years old.

CHAPTER 11

Misery and Abuse

After losing her son, my daughter moved to Virginia, near Washington, DC, to go into treatment for her addiction and other mental problems. I was very pleased and grateful that James agreed to take in my grandson, but it was quite an adjustment for us as a couple and for him. We had only been married for two years and even though Brody had stayed with us numerous times, we hadn't been his legal guardians, so we'd had no control over how to raise him. But because I'd had custody of him before and had raised two children of my own, lack of legal guardianship hadn't stopped me from offering advice to my daughter on how to handle certain child-rearing challenges.

James tried to be a good grandparent but had already proven to have very little patience with Brody during our visitations with him. Also, recently, James had been snapping at me in angry outbursts out of the blue. I knew he was going to have a very rigid parenting style but hadn't expected the anger issues towards Brody that he soon began to exhibit. It was more than just having little patience—James would scream at him any time he disobeyed, was irritated or didn't immediately mind him. The poor kid was only five years old and had recently been removed from his mother; but even without that being part of the mix, I thought James was being too harsh on him. When I would express my displeasure, in private, with the way he was handling his frustration, James would get angry and frustrated with me. He expressed his anger by yelling at me and attacking and insulting my daughter. That was his constant modus operandi: Any time Brody didn't act the way my husband thought he should, I had to listen to a barrage of angry attacks and insults towards my daughter. It was pretty much a daily attack on her.

I couldn't disagree with a lot of what James said about Jessica, but it was difficult listening to his constant insults day after day, year after year. It took a toll on me and on our relationship.

Our dinnertimes were particularly stressful. I came to dread them. James demanded that Brody eat what we cooked, eat it all, use manners, not gulp his drink and not be silly at the table. It's not that I think these are extreme expectations; it was the way he demanded it from him. It was not loving or understanding. James also demanded I cook all fresh food, nothing processed, no more chicken nuggets. None of these requests were wrong or unreasonable from a nutritional standpoint. However, I had a full-time job and didn't get home until 6:30 p.m., later than my husband thought dinner should be served. That definitely caused stress.

James was self-employed at the time, so he could make his own hours. He started doing most of the grocery shopping and then eventually cooking dinner, just because he thought dinner should be served earlier. That was fine with me. He frequently said he didn't mind doing the cooking or shopping but was clearly resentful that he did it. He often said he was doing the "women's work."

That's when I started to get resentful.

At times, something would happen that James didn't like, mostly concerning anything my daughter said or did, and he would go into raging fits towards me. I had seen his short temper and angry outbursts before we were married but I'd overlooked them. The outbursts increased and happened in front of our friends and family. James began to rage over what seemed to most to be very minor irritants, catching others and me off guard and making everyone feel very uncomfortable. He started to complain a lot—about his business, his family, my family, and our friends. He was complaining all the time. I started to see him as a malcontent. No matter how good we had it, he was going to complain. I wish I understood why I allowed myself and my family to be subjected to this abusive treatment. My father was firm and tough on me and my sisters, but he was not abusive and never called us names or made us feel stupid.

About five years into our marriage and three years after we became guardians of our grandson, James was hired to work at a firm but was fired after about two years. He was never happy at this job and came home angry most nights, which created a hostile and uncomfortable environment.

For much of the time after James and I got married, my son had not been in the picture much because he was in jail or doing his thing, so he was rarely interacting with us. By that time, he had been diagnosed with bipolar disorder and prescribed medication. He refused to take the medication and instead began to abuse crystal meth and other illegal drugs. He had been abusing crystal meth daily for years. His brain was fried and he had become extremely delusional. He thought that people controlled him remotely (including me) and that my father was in the CIA and sent him messages in the want ads of *Creatively Loafing*, a local newspaper. Mitchell was really out there, and I tried to keep him and James from having to interact at all. It was always bad when they did and I wasn't always successful in keeping them apart. It was very stressful on us.

About two years after my daughter moved to Virginia, she wanted to come back to Georgia to be closer to her son. I insisted she get into a residential treatment program immediately when she got here. She was accepted into a program and went right into their housing the moment she got off the bus. Jessica had to have a job while there and participate in lots of programs and group activities. She eventually completed their program and was getting her life on track. She spent a lot of time with her son under our supervision.

While in the program, she met and fell in love with her future husband. In 2008, we gave them a wonderful, beautiful wedding at the same place we'd had our wedding. My family and his family were there, and her father and his wife were there. Her father's band played at the reception where he played a song he wrote about her life growing up. It was a wonderful song and well written. Included in the lyrics were many of the fun memories of things she said and did as a child. It was deeply moving. Jessica asked me to help her make a music-video tribute for her father. We did, using pictures I had from my old photo albums. Even my dad's sister, Aunt LuAnn and her husband from Illinois, came for the celebration. Jessica's father was really proud of her—she was so beautiful and humble and grateful on her wedding day. I will remember it always with fond memories.

My dad cried tears of happiness through the entire wedding and reception. It started when she walked down the aisle and her husband-to-be saw her for the first time that day and started bawling his eyes out. Dad was right there with him. It was all I could do to keep it together. I think it's one of the happiest memories for me with her. Brody, who was eight years old, was in the wedding party. He was so happy for his mom and really liked her new husband too.

Shortly after they were married, Brody told me and James that he felt like it was time for them to be together again and asked us if he could move in with them. Jessica was pregnant with their first child and we thought things were going well enough to let him live with his mom and her new husband. It was a difficult and scary transition for us, but Brody told us he was ready and wanted to be part of their family. We agreed to let him go but it was one of the hardest things I've ever done.

After Brody moved in with my daughter and son-in-law, they couldn't do anything right in my husband's eyes. He was angry that they didn't keep Brody active in Tae Kwon Do, which he had been taking for over a year, angry that they didn't follow through on the promises they'd made to get him back. After they lost power in their home for failing to pay the bill, we took them back to court to try to gain custody again. But we lost the case.

James and I managed to struggle through our marriage a few more years but his raging outbursts were increasing and my patience was wearing thin. I put up with it for a long time because he admitted he had a problem, apologized and assured me he was working on the issue. I really wanted to believe things would change but it only got worse.

When my son got out of jail, neither could tolerate each other. My son thought my husband treated me badly—my husband thought my son treated us both badly. The truth was they were both correct and I was a nervous wreck all the time trying to be loving and supportive to my husband and my son while trying to keep the peace. It often felt like I had to choose between them. They were both acting like children having temper tantrums and all I could think about was how badly they were both behaving.

On Christmas day in 2010, they almost got into a fistfight. My position was that they were both wrong in the way they'd handled themselves that morning. James was angry that I didn't support his actions just because he was my husband. What he did that morning was uncalled for and there was no way I could support him. I didn't support what my son did either. It ruined Christmas that year and I believe it was the beginning of the end of our marriage, though it would be another year and a half before he left.

The last year we were together, we went to Cancun, Mexico, with his family to celebrate his parents' sixty-year anniversary. I had hoped it would be a romantic getaway for us at a luxurious resort where we could reunite and be together and find gratitude and forgiveness between us. But what should have been a wonderful and fun-filled week of joy and laughter at this beautiful beach casita was full of tension and discomfort between us.

We tried marriage counseling for about nine months. I think that helped us determine it wasn't going to get better. James was done with the marriage but I thought he really wanted to repair it. I guess he prolonged the agony because he had no income.

We separated after our return from a summer camping trip with Brody. James had been hateful to both of us during that trip, and afterwards Brody expressed to me in private that he did not like the way I was being treated and didn't want to go camping with him again. The truth was I didn't like the way my grandson was being treated, either, and that was the end for me. I asked him to leave that day and told him it was over.

I'm not saying I did nothing wrong: To say my kids were challenging is an understatement, and I didn't always handle that in the best way, though we tried to have loving relationships with them. My daughter and her husband were not responsible with their money and I started financially supporting them too much. I helped them buy two or three cars, helped with food, helped them pay rent sometimes. We had two new grandsons and my daughter was not working. My husband was not happy with the way I was supporting them and I agree I mishandled it.

After James and I decided to divorce, I thought we could end our marriage amicably but I was wrong. It took a year of nasty fighting and expensive legal fees before our divorce was final. I was crushed because I had truly believed we would grow old together, and I really did love the man when we started our marriage, before I found out who he really was.

Soon I began to isolate myself and then I withdrew into depression. I didn't reach out to my friends or even to my sisters very much and I didn't ask for help. My sisters did reach out to me but only two good friends kept checking on me regularly; I am extremely grateful to them for that.

Shortly after my husband left, my dogs, who were now fourteen years old, had become very ill. Levi had dementia and Lisa couldn't get up the stairs due to her severe arthritis. They had never been separated before and I knew it was time to put them to sleep. It was extremely difficult to let them go and after that I felt completely alone for the first time in twenty-five years. One month before our divorce was final, I was about to be faced with another loss, something even worse than losing my husband and my dogs—and I was not prepared for what was to happen next.

CHAPTER 12

The Best Dad in the World

While I was at work one afternoon in June 2012, my stepmother called and said my father had fallen in the bathroom and she had not been able to help him get up. She said he was in a lot of pain and she thought he may have broken his hip. She had called the ambulance and they were now in the emergency room. She told me the X-rays indicated nothing was broken and they were about to send him home. They lived in Chattanooga and it would take me two hours to get there. She said not to worry, that I didn't need to drive up there; she thought he would be fine.

About thirty minutes later, she called again. Her voice was not calm, as it had been before, and all she could say was that something had happened and I needed to get there as quickly as I could. I could tell it was not the time to ask any questions, so I hung up and grabbed my purse and left my office. Without going home first, I drove straight to the hospital in Chattanooga, frantically worried the whole drive. I don't remember if I talked to Kelly (who also lives in Chattanooga) during that drive to the hospital. My heart was beating so fast. I was a nervous wreck and full of fear. Two years prior to this, Dad had suffered a massive stroke and we'd almost lost him then, but he'd recovered after lots of rehab and hard work on his part.

I couldn't believe that after surviving that stroke two years earlier, a fall in the bathroom would be the thing that got him. We were also dealing with his skin cancer. Dad had severe skin cancer through his entire adult life. In the last ten years, he'd had to see his doctor more and more frequently. At this time, he was seeing his skin doctor every six weeks so he could inspect Dad's body for new growths. Just prior to his fall, his doctor had found a melanoma on Dad's forehead and he was scheduled for its surgical removal three days after that fall. My poor dad had been cut on in so many places that his arms, face, ears and neck were scarred all over from having cancers removed. They had run out of places to graft skin from. He was very weary of all that cutting. He was eighty-one years old when he fell in June 2012.

My sisters and I were very close to our dad, who had been a wonderful father and role model. He loved us all very much, too, and we knew it and felt it throughout our lives. His family always came first, no matter what.

When I got to the hospital, I was directed to the CCU. My stepmom and sister Kelly were there and told me what had happened. Right after my stepmom had called me the first time saying he was about to go home, Dad lay back on the bed of the ER, his eyes rolled back into his head and he flatlined.

This caught the entire ER staff off guard but they immediately began CPR on him. After nineteen minutes of them trying to bring him back, the doctor told my stepmom it was time to let him go. She asked to be allowed back into the room (they had run her out while they worked on him) to say good-bye. When she got in there, the doctor said they had a pulse, so they took him to CCU, intubated him and put him on various life-support machines. No one really knew how much damage was done to his brain, his heart or his body after nineteen minutes of being dead, and it looked pretty grim. I couldn't believe what was happening and we were all in shock.

They had just returned from an Alaskan cruise a week earlier. That was one of the things on Dad's bucket list and he'd had so much fun on that cruise. I had seen him a few days before they'd left for the cruise and he hadn't seemed to be getting around very well. He had been having trouble with his feet. I'd wondered if he was going to be able to get around on that ship, but when my sister had picked them up at the airport after the cruise, she'd said he was like a different man, so happy and enthusiastic and moving and walking like a new man. He'd been so thrilled that the trip had been fantastic. His first cousin, Chuck, had gone with them and the three of them had had a wonderful time. Dad had been on cloud nine.

He had fallen two days before Father's Day so when Father's Day came, we were all there with him taking turns going into the room in CCU to see if he was conscious. I went in with my stepmom. Dad had a tube down his throat, so he couldn't talk, and his eyes were closed. I was holding his hand and rubbing his forehead with a cool, damp cloth. He suddenly opened his eyes and looked at us, then he slowly lifted his hand, which had an IV attached to a medicine bag hanging on a pole, and put his finger on the spot on his forehead where he had the melanoma. My stepmom and I knew it was his way of asking if he'd had the surgery to have it removed. He'd been unconscious for a couple of days, and he didn't realize why he was there or what had happened.

At that moment, we knew he had not suffered brain damage from having flatlined for nineteen minutes. We rejoiced that he wasn't brain dead and explained to him why he was there. We could tell he understood as best he could, and for the next few days he was in and out of consciousness but I think he mostly knew what was going on around him. He didn't like the tube in his throat. A line in his leg going to his heart measured how many breaths he was taking.

After a few days, his cardiologist told us that over fifty percent of his heart had been damaged and that his chances of surviving were maybe twenty percent. But Dad's a fighter and several days later, they took him off life support and took the tube out and he rallied. They moved him to a regular room and said he might survive.

Dad's cardiologist knew him personally as a friend and knew what a fighter he was. That doctor gave us hope that Dad might survive this; it had been five days since he'd gone to the ER.

During the following week, his sister and her son and daughter were able to come visit him. Dad was so excited to see them and could even talk to them a little bit. He always loved and enjoyed all my cousins so much. He was as proud of them as he was of us. I know my other cousins held him in their hearts but were not able to come to see him. I am extremely grateful so many friends and family members got to see him that week.

Soon we got the heartbreaking news that the doctors had found a serious blood clot in his leg that they did not believe he could recover from—and he had pneumonia and was not doing well in general. The doctors were now talking about moving him to a hospice room the next morning. When I heard "hospice" I began to understand how bad it was. My sisters, our stepmom, and I were devastated and heartbroken but still couldn't believe we would lose him.

When I walked into his room the night before we moved him to hospice, he was awake and aware of his surroundings and knew who was there with him. Kelly had just left and Christy was staying with him for the night. He looked at me and smiled such a peaceful, calming smile, and I knew he knew what was happening. I could feel he was ready to go. I put my arms around his neck, hugged him, and told him how much I loved him and what a great father he was and how lucky I was to be his daughter. I thanked him for everything he'd taught me, put my head on his shoulder, my arm around his neck and hugged him and held him and sent him so much love through the energies of our bodies that I knew he could feel my love and admiration. He put his arm around my neck and told me with his eyes and his expression that he loved me. I knew with every fiber of my being that he understood what I was telling him, how much I loved him, and that he knew it was our good-bye.

I then ran out to the hall and completely broke down, leaning on the wall and sinking down to the floor. I just lost it.

That was the last time we communicated. The next morning, we wheeled him around the corner on the same floor to a hospice room. They gave him some morphine. The hospice doctor came in and told us she didn't know how long it would take but would be soon. My sisters, our stepmom, and I stayed with him all day, holding his hand and talking to him and giving him our love. My daughter also came to say good-bye. Later that evening, with all four of us around him, he took his last breath. It was June 29, 2012. We were all brave and strong for him—we knew he was ready. It had been in his eyes. I'm so proud of how courageous we all were that evening. I was extremely grateful he left us feeling no pain and I know he was met by his parents in the next dimension and they all rejoiced to be together again.

We buried him at the National Cemetery in Chattanooga, Tennessee. He'd had it all set up years before. He had planned his whole funeral and had already asked his three best friends to speak at it. He had even recorded the music he wanted played: three different versions of "His Eye Is on the Sparrow," two versions without words and one with the words. A song his father had loved and also wanted played at his funeral. It was all exactly what he wanted and exactly what he had written down and prearranged. It was a celebration of love and remembrance.

He is with me and the others in my family always; and I am forever a part of him.

CHAPTER 13

The Love of Her Life

Mom met James "Jim" D. Guler around 1990 after placing a series of personal ads in a newspaper, to meet men available for companionship. They went on a few dates and hit it off quickly, immediately drawn to each other. Mom was working as a live-in nanny for two small children at the time. She was fifty-eight years old and wasn't very happy. She wanted friends and fun and was really missing companionship. Jim lived alone in a large, beautiful Tudor-style home on Lake Lanier with lake frontage and a boat dock in a nice cove. Jim owned and ran a dry-dock marina that he'd had for many years. He worked on all the boats as a mechanic and took care of all the business basically by himself. He never had children of his own but had a brother, two nephews and a niece. He was seven years younger than Mom but you couldn't tell it because Mom still looked great for her age. They each had something the other needed at that time in their lives.

Mom was a great homemaker and she loved being at home and generally filling that role. Jim needed someone to cook for him, clean and decorate his house, and take care of him. It was a perfect fit for them both, so it wasn't long before she moved in with him. I think they loved each other very much, early on, and Mom told us numerous times that Jim was "the love of her life." My sisters and I wanted her to be happy and wanted to know she would be taken care of so she wouldn't be worrying about earning an income, which caused her a great deal of stress. It seemed perfect—but we didn't really know Jim yet.

It didn't take long for us to realize that Jim had a few "quirks" and didn't mind telling anyone all about himself. In fact, his ego was so large that he wanted everyone to know about his days with the Ku Klux Klan, his certified Nazi memorabilia collection, his German gun and music collections, and his silver collection. He believed that the Caucasian race was superior to African-Americans and to most other races.

To us, it was obvious early on that Jim suffered obsessive-compulsive disorder. He was a gun enthusiast and made his own ammunition. We found out later that he had hidden guns all around—in the couches, bed tables, cars, and more places.

He never considered what anyone else ever needed (unless it was a drink refill). He did what he wanted regardless of how obnoxious he was to other people. He liked to drink, a lot, and party—it was a great party house. He invited his neighbors over frequently to have fun. When he had too much to drink, he would talk about his vulgar sexcapades and embarrass Mother at the dinner table or anywhere else he wanted to open his mouth and brag.

Personality-wise, I never really saw how Mom could put up with him, but for the next twenty-three years she did. She took good care of him and his home, and she made it seem to us as if she was happy and being taken care of, as well. They bought nice furniture and she decorated his home with tasteful accessories from the '90s that stood the test of time. They never married and never had the intent between them to be married, so they never met the legal requirements for a common-law marriage.

Jim was very controlling of who came into the house. He was controlling over the thermostat and kept the house quite warm during the summer months, and he was particular about how many fans could be plugged in. Even when they had guests to spend the night, he refused to allow a comfortable temperature for everyone. But we never saw Jim yell at our mother or show abusive behavior, and Mother was never afraid of him and never felt that her life was in danger.

As they got older, and Jessica had three children, we didn't visit them often because Jim didn't like children and didn't want them anywhere in the house or yard unsupervised. We went at Christmas because that was Mom's favorite holiday and she liked to cook Christmas dinner for the whole family. My sisters would come in from Tennessee and Colorado to be with her and I would take my family. We had a good celebration with them at least one time of year. We always knew that Mom bought the Christmas food and presents with her own money (her social security) and that Jim never spent a dime on Christmas gifts for any of us no matter how many we gave him over the years. We really didn't care, but it didn't go unnoticed.

Jim retired about eighteen years into their relationship and sold his marina business. A few years after retiring he was diagnosed with stage 4 colon cancer. He underwent surgery to have his colon removed. All three of us girls went to the hospital to help him get well enough to go home by encouraging him to get up and walk around the hospital floor with us and to just get out of the bed and be more active. He had gotten depressed because he now had to have a colostomy bag and he was in the hospital for over a month.

Then Mom, who suffered from atrial fibrillation, had further heart problems and was hospitalized several times. Eventually she was given a pacemaker. After that, Jim had a minor stroke and never fully recovered from it. We know Mom was getting frustrated with the changes in Jim's abilities to handle his household responsibilities and his inability to take care of things the way he had done for twenty-three years. Neither was healthy enough to take care of that house, but they also didn't like people being in the house even if it was to help them. Jim didn't want anyone there to see how his mind had deteriorated, so they began to talk about selling it and moving to an assisted-living facility.

Sad to say, Jim was so obsessed with the house that he kept changing his mind about selling it. He began to get paranoid about his next-door neighbors and thought they were spying on him through his computer and thought they were to blame for a water-drainage problem. Mom and Jim's relationship began to deteriorate too and she was exasperated with her situation. For the first time since she'd been with Jim, she told my sister Christy she wanted to leave him. She wanted him to give her enough money to move into an assisted-living apartment on her own. But then a few days later she called my sister again saying they had made up and everything was fine. But soon we found it wasn't fine and what happened next would change my and my sisters' lives forever.

CHAPTER 14

"He's got a gun."

In the early morning hours of August 28, 2013, I received a telephone call at about 4:30 from my sister Christy. I thought I was dreaming because what she said next made me feel that I was in the middle of a nightmare. She had received a call from a Gwinnett County police detective. He told her that Jim had shot and killed Mother, then killed himself—they were both dead and lying in their driveway. He said it happened right in front of a Gwinnett County officer who had responded to a 911 call from Mom stating her "husband" had a gun and was breaking into her bedroom. Within about four minutes, the responding police officer came down their street and parked by the mailbox. When the officer got out of his car, he saw them standing towards the bottom of the steeply pitched driveway. The officer began walking towards them with his gun drawn. It was 12:30 a.m. Mom only said one thing to the officer: "He's got a gun." The officer could see Jim standing behind her but could not see his hands. The policeman told Jim to show his hands, but instead of putting his hands up, Jim shot Mom in the back at point-blank range. She fell and hit the concrete, landing on her back. The officer then fired at Jim, hitting him in the foot, causing him to fall and hit the driveway. As the officer was walking towards them, Jim lifted his .357 magnum, aimed it towards his chest and shot himself.

I couldn't believe my ears. Surely I was just having a horrible nightmare and I'll soon wake up and things will all be back to normal. I mean Mom is eighty years old and Jim is seventy-three. How many rich, elderly couples living in an affluent neighborhood die in a murder/suicide? I wondered to myself. I sat up in bed and asked, "What did you say?" Then she told me the story again, adding that they were still lying dead in their driveway and that the homicide detective had just called about what had happened and were waiting for the coroner to arrive.

Now I was in shock, trying to process the words coming out of her mouth. This just can't be real—it's got to be some kind of cruel joke, surely. But no, it was really happening. I asked Christy if she knew anything else, like why or what happened, but she didn't. I just kept saying, "Oh, my God," over and over again.

Christy had been here in Georgia at their house a month ago and Mom had been frustrated that Jim was unable to take care of household responsibilities (paying bills, taking out the trash, and so on) and frustrated that he was forgetful and didn't want *anyone* in the house. But he had not been acting violent, and Christy insisted Mom was not in fear of him in any way.

Christy then gave me the detective's name and telephone number. I called and talked to him. The detective confirmed what Christy told me but didn't provide any more information except that Jim's nephew had arrived at the scene, but it's all taped off and he can't get close to them.

The detective told me they didn't know why it happened, only that the coroner should arrive soon. If he asked me any questions, I don't remember them. I hung up and thought that Mom had been lying dead on the cold, hard driveway for almost five hours now, because it happened at around 12:30 a.m. She died all alone with no one there to hold her hand and say good-bye or tell her that it's okay or that they love her. I couldn't imagine what was going through her head when it happened or how horrified and scared she must have felt. I was stunned and frozen, not knowing what to do next or how to feel.

I couldn't even cry yet, I was in such shock.

I'd had foot surgery three weeks earlier to remove a heel spur, so I was on a medical leave of absence from work. Still wearing a soft boot on my right foot, I was not able to drive and nor was my son. I wanted to get in that car and drive to their house an hour away and be by Mom's side so she wouldn't be alone.

I got up and walked to the top of the basement stairs where my son was sleeping in the basement bedroom. Mitchell had been living with me for four months, after being paroled in April. I called to him. I yelled that something terrible has happened. When he came upstairs, I told him what had happened. He was also in shock. I sat down in my living room chair and turned on the TV, wondering if it's on the news.

It was. It was all over every local news channel about the elderly couple in Buford who died hours ago in what appears to be a murder/suicide.

The reporters were standing on the street in front of Mom and Jim's house, updating the situation for the public, while behind them you see the flashing lights, fire trucks, first responders, ambulance, police cars, and yellow tape, along with reporters from other networks. My son was freaking out. I was freaking out. I could hardly believe what was happening or what I was watching. It felt as if I was in a horror movie, watching it unfold. We flipped channels and it was on every major station at 5:00 in the morning.

This continued for several hours and we received our status updates from the television. At first, they reported that a neighbor had said police had been there before for domestic violence. I thought, *Really? That's news to me.* Eventually, they did their homework and reported no history of calls to the house for domestic disputes.

I then called my daughter, who was in shock and couldn't believe what was happening. She was on her way over. I called Kelly or she called me, I can't remember which, and she said that she was getting in her car to head down from Chattanooga within the next hour.

She was obviously in shock and disbelief, fuming at Jim— we both were—and were both trying to figure out what happened since Christy was there thirty days ago. Christy had talked to Mom on the phone two weeks before this. Mom had first said Jim and she were fighting and then said things were fine and "not to worry."

Neither Kelly nor I would have ever thought this could have happened, that Jim could do this. In a lot of ways, Mom's temper was worse than Jim's. As Kelly and I were discussing the situation, we both realized all the complex legal ramifications we could be facing from this. She suggested we might want to hire an attorney. None of us have ever dealt with handling someone's estate. Our stepmom handled our dad's estate. Especially under these circumstances, we needed to be prepared for what might happen next. I agreed because I had no clue what would happen next. We were both in major shock and knew we will need help getting through this.

It was 6:00 a.m. and Kelly would soon arrive at my house from Tennessee. I was shaking from my nerves and still in shock, but my mind was racing. I wanted to start doing things. But what could I do? I couldn't drive to Mom's. Yet, I could call my boss, who was legal counsel for a major corporation, an internationally known company. At the time, I was a paralegal in their litigation department. I explained what happened and asked if he could recommend anyone who could help us. He called back within an hour and gave me the name of a civil attorney.

That was the beginning of an excellent relationship with a wonderful attorney who was not only good at handling wrongful death cases, but who's got heart and soul. He cares. By the time I talked to him, he'd seen the news, knew what had happened, and knew a lot about the man who'd killed my mother. No words can describe how important he was in helping us handle the situation right from the start to the end. He brought in an estate attorney, an expert on probate issues, because this was probably going to get complex. I honestly don't know what we would have done without these two attorneys.

In the hours that followed, I tried to process what was happening, what I needed to do next, whom I needed to call. And I kept going back to how it had all happened. I was trying not to focus on how horrified Mom must have been, standing there in the driveway with a madman behind her holding a gun in her back. We'd never seen Jim get violent, ever, and I was trying to make sense of it.

I talked to Christy in Denver. She was trying to get a flight to Atlanta as soon as possible.

When Kelly arrived, we tried to comfort each other and immediately began speculating about what had happened that led up to this horrible event.

My daughter arrived, too, and the three of us started calling funeral homes and getting information. Were we going to cremate her or bury her? Kelly said Mom had wanted to be cremated. So we started to gather information while the horror of what was happening was starting to sink in.

I've since learned this is what happens to all survivors of suicides and homicides: We started asking ourselves "Why?" Why did this happen, were there signs, what did we miss, what should we have done differently, who can we blame besides the obvious?

We knew we needed to get into the house and find Mom's will, her purse, her address book, her checkbook…what else? It was all too much to think about…how were we going to get through this? Eventually, I would be able to say the answer to the last question is "together"—we got through it together.

Soon we learned...from the news stations...that the coroner had arrived and the bodies were finally being removed from the driveway and taken to the morgue. Something's just not right about waiting for your mother's body to be picked up from the cold hard concrete and taken to the morgue. Learning what's going on from the news reporter on television was like adding salt to the wound, but I was grateful they were finally being moved. My heart was just aching from knowing this was happening, but aching even more that I couldn't be, and wasn't, there with her, even though there was nothing I could have done. The detective had said the scene was blocked off and no one could get close to the bodies.

Later in the morning, the detective called again, asked a few questions and gave us the number of the forensic investigator at the morgue. He said they would let us know when the body would be released. The detective asked me a few questions about Mom and Jim and told me he'd released the murder scene and house to Jim's nephew, Mark. I answered his few questions as best as I could about what we knew had been happening between them prior to this, but it was nothing new to him. He told me I could contact Mark about gaining entry to the house to get whatever we needed. He also told me to call him if we had any problems getting in the house. He said protocol required them to leave the home in a family member's custody. He also told me that Mark was not very helpful or forthcoming with any information and had not said much. Additionally, the detective told me Mark informed him that my sisters and I were not close to our mother. That was astonishing because we had never even met Mark in twenty-three years and we knew for a fact he was not close to Mom or Jim. So it was unclear why he said or even thought that, but I think Mark found out pretty quickly that couldn't have been further from the truth.

Over the last year, Jim had been having some problems functioning, remembering words, and communicating. He frequently appeared confused and was embarrassed for anyone to see his symptoms for fear people would think he was "stupid." He hadn't wanted anyone (including us) in his home to see how he was acting. So Mom had been pushing us away the year before this happened to keep Jim happy. My sister Christy had received a call from Jim a month before the murder, telling her that Mom was really upset and threatening to leave him. Then when Mom and Christy had talked, Mom had asked Christy to visit them when she came to my house for our summer vacation the last week of July.

Christy did visit them and could see that Jim was very frustrated about his current health status. He kept saying he felt stupid because he couldn't communicate as he always had and was having problems eating. She spent the night with them and talked to Mom alone for hours, leaving early the next day to come to my house to spend the week with Kelly and me. Christy had said Mom did not ask for help from any of us and was not fearful of Jim in any way.

We were all frustrated with Mom that she was pushing us away when it appeared she really needed our help and support the most. It was clear she was trying to work everything out herself. Mom always wanted things to appear fine and if they didn't appear fine, she wanted us to believe she could handle it. What we learned later from Jim's autopsy report was that his cancer had returned and had metastasized in his liver. He was essentially a walking dead man at that time, but neither of them had told us that. We don't know if they had known it at the time, though I don't see how Jim couldn't have known.

We did find out from their neighbor (Mom hadn't told us) that Jim had been in the hospital the week prior to the shooting, but the neighbor didn't know why. She said Mom had been very active during that week, leaving the house every day. That was unusual because they were pretty reclusive and normally she didn't leave the house that much, so it was noted by the neighbor. We don't really know where Mom was going when she left the house that week—she could have been going to the hospital to visit Jim. But we discovered through papers we found in the house that she had been meeting with salespeople who'd been showing her assisted-living residences.

CHAPTER 15

The Heirs

What followed this tragedy was an intensely painful journey settling the wrongful death claim our mother's estate had against Jim's estate. This involved difficult interactions with Jim's heirs over the course of the following year.

We called Jim's nephew, Mark, that first day and left a message that we needed to get inside the house to get Mom's will and purse and other things. But his nephew wouldn't call us back. After leaving several messages, we had to call the detective to intervene and get the nephew to call us back. Finally, Mark called, wanting to know why we needed to get in the house. Our response was "What do you mean why do we need to get inside the house?" He acted as if he had no idea why we would need to get to Mom's belongings. After we explained it to him, he agreed to set an appointment for us to go there the next day. We had a clear sense this was not going to go well and we were incensed and knew something wasn't right about his attitude.

It only went downhill from there.

The next day, we were supposed to meet Jim's nephews at the house at 1:30 p.m. However, the morning of our meeting we received a telephone call about 9:00 a.m. from the neighbor next door to Mom and Jim's, very upset. She told us the nephews had been at the house all morning and she had been watching them load up things from inside the house and drive off with them in their truck. This neighbor loved our mom and had called us before when Mom had been taken to the hospital in an ambulance. She was not very fond of Jim's nephews. On hearing what the nephews had been doing, I decided to call our attorney, who we were scheduled to meet that morning at 10:00, and he told me they should not be doing that. Kelly was furious and wanted to drive to Mom and Jim's house right then. Our attorney suggested he call the nephew we had been communicating with and make it clear that they should not be removing items from the house, and we agreed that was a good idea. So he called, saying he was calling on our behalf and asked if they had an attorney. Mark refused to answer that question, but he made it clear he wasn't concerned about whether or not he should be removing property from the house. After hearing that, we all agreed that instead of us meeting our attorneys at 10:00 at my house, we needed to drive out to Mom's house in Buford and try to stop the nephews from removing any further items from the house.

Kelly wanted to leave immediately, so she got in her car and left by herself before Christy and I were ready. The attorneys suggested that it would probably be helpful if they came along, and we wholeheartedly agreed. When Kelly and the attorneys got to Mom's house, she went right up to the door and rang the doorbell. One of the nephews came to the door and, seeing who it was, barely opened it, telling her she couldn't come inside because it was not the scheduled time we had set up to be there. They wouldn't open the door for her except for a little crack. Kelly then introduced our attorneys, who were standing on the sidewalk a few feet behind her, to which the man at the door responded that they would not be allowed access to the house at all—only we could go inside at the scheduled time.

Now, my sister is not shy or soft-spoken, plus she was already upset at the lack of respect these guys were showing, considering the fact that their uncle murdered our mother two days prior. We were traumatized and had been through quite a lot. Kelly had no tolerance for the lack of cooperation and the disrespect being shown to us. When they told her she couldn't go in until our meeting time, which was three-and-a-half hours later, she pushed the door open and walked in saying, "Oh yes I can. I have just as much right to be here as you do. This was our mother's house too and she lived here for twenty-three years." Our attorneys were standing on the sidewalk watching this unfold. This was their first meeting with Kelly or any of us and I'm sure they were curious about how this was all going to play out. They decided to call Christy and me—we were almost there—to give us an update on what was happening at the house.

When we got the call, Christy and I couldn't believe what we were hearing. We were asking each other why Jim's nephews would be acting that way. What did they think we were going to do, ransack the place? I mean, *really*, it was bizarre. Christy and I were saying to each other, "Go, Kelly!!!"

Once she got inside the house one of the nephews told Kelly that he was the executor of Jim's estate and was in charge of the house. This had little effect on Kelly's attitude because she really didn't care about that at that point. She walked into the kitchen, knowing exactly where Mom had kept her purse, but it was not there. She then asked one of them where Mom's purse was. They played dumb and started following her as she went from room to room looking for Mom's purse.

Kelly then made a major decision: She went to the front door and told our attorneys, very insistently, that she wanted them to come inside because she was not going to be intimidated by these three men following her around while she looked for our mother's important things.

So they went inside and again asked the nephews if they had an attorney, to which they replied yes. Lo and behold, our attorney knew their attorneys' firm and was working with one of their attorneys on another case, so he had the telephone number in his cell phone. He called, got one of their attorneys on the phone immediately, and explained that we had hired them to represent us in our wrongful death claim against Jim's estate, and then he explained what was going on at the house.

Their attorney indicated to ours that he had no idea this was happening or that we had an appointment to get into the house that day, or he would have been there himself. (Clearly, the nephews didn't think it necessary to tell them.) So our attorney explained that we had gotten a call from the neighbor, that she had observed the nephews removing property from the house earlier that morning. He explained that had prompted our early arrival but Jim's nephews had refused to let us in the house. Their attorney then asked to speak to his clients. He told them to let us all in and let us do what we needed to do. He also told our attorney that he would instruct his clients not to remove any property from the house.

By then Christy and I had arrived and for the next several hours, we went through Mother's bedroom and other parts of the house looking through drawers for her will and other things. They'd had separate bedrooms for years due to Jim's snoring. The first thing we noticed was a metal bar lying on the floor by her bedroom door. The kind of bar you put under the doorknob to jam the door from being opened from the other side. When the three of us saw that, we knew she had been trying to keep Jim out of her room. None of us had any idea she'd gone to such lengths, had needed to take *any* measures, to protect herself from him. Seeing that bar, and knowing how that night had ended, sent chills down our backs.

We would later listen to her 911 call. We heard Mom telling the operator that her husband was busting through the door to her room, that he was mad and had a gun.

At that point, understanding what that bar meant, I was shaking and in a daze. I was hoping our attorneys were looking for and finding everything we needed because I could hardly think and still couldn't believe what was happening. I was hobbling around that huge house slowly with a boot on my foot (it had been three weeks since my surgery), smelling Mom's clothes and blankets and trying to deal with all my emotions.

We found her will and other papers and the attorneys took pictures of everything in her room, but we never found her address book, checkbook or purse. Kelly noticed that the Keurig coffee maker Christy had given them for Christmas was not in the kitchen and that Mom's perfume and other personal items from her bathroom were missing. Everything in Mom's bathroom had been moved around; nothing was the way she'd kept it. Kelly knew where Mom had kept everything. She knew how and where Mom had kept her perfume, hairbrushes and makeup, but nothing was where it was supposed to be. So we asked her to look through the house to see what else was missing.

I am speculating, but it seemed clear to us that these guys had gone through the whole house, including Mom's personal belongings. We didn't know what they'd taken, what they'd moved, why they'd moved it or why they would've touched anything of our mother's before we got there. And her will was sitting inside a drawer in an envelope placed neatly on top of her clothing just waiting for us to open the drawer and find it right there on top. I'm absolutely sure that's not how our mother would have left it. Talk about adding insult to injury. We were all three trying to imagine if the roles had been reversed how we would have handled the situation. We would have had more empathy and understanding for them. We would never go through someone else's personal belongings and we darn sure wouldn't have started removing property from the house. It felt as though we were being violated and victimized again and it hadn't even been two full days since this had all started.

Mom and Jim had both told us that he had left everything to her in his will and that she had left everything to him in her will. Eventually we learned that the will we found was null and void because she had not gotten two people to witness her signature, a requirement in the State of Georgia. We eventually saw the copy of Jim's will that left Mom everything, but it didn't have two witness signatures either, so it was invalid. For years Mom had told us she would be taken care of in the event of Jim's death. That had been an extremely important issue to her and we knew it. Jim had told me personally years prior that he was leaving everything to her in his will. As I mentioned earlier, Jim had sold his dry-dock marina business on Lake Lanier to retire several years prior to his death. He'd said he had invested the money from the sale in IRAs and other investment vehicles and that Mom was the beneficiary on most of those accounts.

Soon we would find out things were very different from what we had always been told but for that moment, we were trying to find everything we needed to deal with her death, her burial and her wishes. It was a time of deep despair, sadness, frustration, hurt and anger. I couldn't understand how it had come to this. I kept thinking about her using items to keep him out of her bedroom, not just that night but other nights before that. I couldn't understand how or why we didn't know. Mom was a strong-willed and strong-minded woman. She wouldn't tolerate abuse, or so I had thought. She hadn't told anyone about it or asked for help. I was trying to come to terms with my experience and knowledge of domestic violence from the ten years prior work with victims of such violence and how I didn't know she was having to block him from entering her bedroom or know about other violence that might have been occurring in that home. It was a devastating blow that I still think about.

After that initial entry into the house, we requested access to obtain her Christmas decorations and the ornaments she had collected since our childhood; instead they packed them up and delivered them to their attorney's office for me to pick up there, but we never found the ornaments we made as children. We requested access at a later time to identify her personal property and belongings for inventory purposes. Again, we were denied. We were never granted access to that house again by Jim's heirs for any reason.

CHAPTER 16

The Great Change
of Beneficiary Mystery

The heirs of Jim's estate appeared to have zero sympathy or empathy for us or our mother. We found out why pretty quickly. Apparently, merely a few hours before Jim killed our mother, he had changed his will, cutting her completely out of it. Mom and Jim had gone to his attorney's office hours earlier the same day as the murder, and the attorney explained the changes to them and afterwards Jim signed it. The new will left everything to his brother, two nephews and a niece, his only heirs. The heirs knew the night the murder happened about the signing of the new will that day and knew Jim was going to change the beneficiary of his accounts from my mother to them.

They also knew Jim had significant amounts of cash in the various accounts and investments for which they knew my mother was the beneficiary at the time of his death. Jim had been in the process of signing multiple Change of Beneficiary forms that day but (I'm assuming here, based on information we received from an account agent) had not sent them back to his broker or account representative yet.

So what did the "new beneficiaries" do with these forms that had not been delivered to the broker by Jim Guler? We learned from the account agent that the new beneficiaries personally delivered the Change of Beneficiary forms to him at his office. We also learned, by having handwriting experts review the forms, that Jim had changed the beneficiaries the four heirs named above, and that he had only signed the forms. He had not personally filled out any of the other information on the forms; the nephews filled out the paperwork.

Now think about that for a minute... Jim had not sent in the change forms himself before he died and they were dated the day of his death. The new beneficiaries hand carried those forms to the agent's office — *after* Jim was dead. You don't have to be a rocket scientist to think something was very fishy with that picture. Amazingly, the agent accepted the forms and even asked if they wanted to file a claim. Thankfully, their attorney had advised them not to file the claim for the payout, knowing there would be issues with not just the way the forms were submitted, I presume, but also due to the wrongful death claim.

Another interesting fact about these change forms: *We were never told about them by the heirs or their attorney at any time during our settlement negotiations.* We had been given the account statements for four months prior to Jim's death, something they had agreed to provide during settlement negotiations. We could never get a straight answer from their side as to whether Mom was beneficiary of the accounts. The only thing we were told was that the beneficiary was "in the process of being changed." That was in the first days after the tragedy and it was never discussed again.

The account agent's name was on the statements, so I called him and asked him point-blank, "Who is the beneficiary for Jim's accounts?" I explained who I was and the agent understood exactly who I was because he'd known Mom and Jim. He told me he had been to their house and was a personal friend. He expressed his sympathy and told me how shocked and sorry he was about what happened. He then told me the heirs named in Jim's new will were the beneficiaries. He informed me that Mom had been the beneficiary prior to the change. This was new information to me and I wondered how they had become the new beneficiaries so quickly after Jim had signed the new will. I could tell that the agent was starting to get uncomfortable with my probing questions, so I explained that I was going to have my attorney call him.

I called my attorney, who was very interested in the information I had just received. He called the agent and talked for quite a while. He learned how it all went down the day Jim died, how his heirs had e-mailed the agent to inform him of Jim's death and that they would be bringing the Change of Beneficiary forms to his office later that day.

We found out about these forms approximately four months after the deaths occurred. We did get a copy of them after learning of their existence from the agent. We had already agreed to try to mediate the case in an attempt to settle our claim against the estate, but it had not been scheduled yet when we learned of these change forms. Finding out about the forms' existence and how they had been handled changed everything for us from then on. We didn't volunteer the fact that we had found out about these forms to their estate attorneys and they certainly hadn't informed us about their existence, either. I assumed they were going to tell us that Mom was not the beneficiary of the accounts at some point during our negotiations but clearly they were in no hurry. So the first thing I thought about when we found out about these change forms was "Why would they want to hide that information from us?" I mean, if everything was on the up-and-up and properly executed, why not tell us right off the bat that Jim had changed the beneficiaries the day he died?

The reason the beneficiary issue was so critical to our case is this: If Jim's heirs were the legal beneficiaries, then the money in the accounts would be passed on directly to the heirs and would not ever become part of Jim's estate. Our wrongful death claim was against his estate and therefore only applied to what was owned by the estate.

Soon we found out what they were using as their defense tactic. Their attorney had to find some kind of defense to save his clients from losing their inheritance, so what he came up with was "Don't punish the heirs for something they didn't do."

Oh boy, was he kidding?

Their uncle and brother killed our mother, it's his estate, and the message to us was we shouldn't punish them for something Jim had done. It was hard to fathom the message that even though our mom was the victim of a brutal murder, we shouldn't try to seek justice on her behalf. The truth was it just didn't matter to them how they treated us because they weren't the ones who killed our mother and besides, their uncle was dead. They were going to do what they wanted and to hell with how it looked or how hurtful it was to us.

Over the next twelve months we prepared to mediate and settle this case. Though they'd agreed early on to provide a complete inventory of what was in the house, they did not do that. Jim had collected cars and guns. Three cars that had been in the basement of the house, along with a motorcycle and numerous guns, had all been removed from the house. Jim had made his own ammunition. The ammunition-making machine that had been in his shop disappeared and was never mentioned. They never told us what they took out of the house and never provided a complete inventory of the years, makes or models of the cars or of the guns in the two large gun safes they'd removed, so we couldn't determine their value.

They brought in an appraiser, who took pictures of the itemized property in the house and put a fair-market value of the items next to the pictures. However, we thought the appraiser's report was extremely unprofessional and poorly done.

We will never know why Jim picked that day to change the will. We will never know why Jim didn't help Mom prepare a new will along with his. We do know it had been extremely important to Mom that she be taken care of upon Jim's death. We know he'd promised to take care of her after his death and we know Mom would not have agreed to being cut out of his will without some other promise from him to support her. We have speculated that he had promised to give her something else to get her to go along with the changes he'd made in the attorney's office without her raising hell about it. We've also speculated that she might have had some information about him that she'd threatened to use against him.

It's possible that whatever he agreed to give her, he changed his mind, causing an argument between them that evening. It's also possible he gave her a large sum of money then wanted it back. I wouldn't be surprised if his nephews knew more than they told us. We were told in mediation that one of the nephews had come into town from Florida a few days before the killing to help Mom or Jim or both find an assisted-living place to move into. If all of Jim's nephews were in town the day of the murder and the will change, then it's highly likely they knew what Jim was doing that day including knowing they were now going to be the heirs or beneficiaries to his estate. Remember they filled out the forms for Jim to sign. If the heirs knew any more about what happened that night, I don't believe they would ever tell us.

It is interesting to me that when one nephew was questioned by the homicide detective the night it happened, he didn't mention that Jim had cut Mom out of his will just a few hours before the murder/suicide. Recall that the investigator had told me the nephew was not very helpful when he was questioned the night it all happened. Because Jim shot her in front of the police, there was no question about that. So I guess it was not really important to them, ultimately, why he did it.

Our mother had taken care of their uncle and that house for twenty-three years. She'd loved him, cooked for him, and looked after him. She'd cleaned the house and done his laundry. We were damn sure not going to let him get away with her murder and not pay for what he did to her. When we heard the 911 tape, there was no doubt that she had suffered and was afraid for her life. We believe that while she stood in that driveway, with a gun in her back, she probably knew she was going to die. That's something we have to live with the rest of our lives and no amount of money will make that go away.

CHAPTER 17

The Ripple Effects

We will forever be haunted by not knowing what led up to this murder, but we will accept the fact we will never know why he did it. It wouldn't really change anything for us other than merely knowing why she died, and we have to accept that.

Almost a full year after the murder, we did eventually reach a settlement at a mediation that lasted over ten hours. We agreed to take their house and the property "left" in it, along with the pontoon boat that was in the boat dock. For whatever reason, none of us felt negative vibes or bad energy in that house. Mother had loved the house and we think she would have been happy that her estate won it in the end.

It didn't take long to sell the house that spring and it was such a relief to have it all behind us. We had spent so much time and energy dealing with Jim's family and getting the case settled that we had not had time to grieve her death. Plus, after having her cremated, we had not had the memorial service we planned to have for Mom, so her ashes had been sitting in my living room and we hadn't decided what to do with them. We hadn't been able to make those decisions during the stressful period we'd spent dealing with her estate.

We eventually bought a marble bench to hold her cremains and picked a spot under a tree in a beautiful garden area of a cemetery near my house. The bench can hold the cremains of three people, so my sister Christy and I decided to have our cremains interred in the same bench so Mom wouldn't be alone. We had the bench engraved, had a service and finally interred her ashes.

I'm very grateful to be able to say that those twelve months of pain and suffering dealing with Jim's family resulted in my sisters and me being closer than we have ever been. We didn't agree on everything, but we didn't fight, argue or hurt each other. We listened to and loved each other and stayed open-minded.

Losing both our parents so close together, and under the conditions in which we lost them, made us realize our mortality. That life is short and we shouldn't waste it fighting and living in resentment. I know our parents would be proud of us for the way we handled their deaths and that is our gift to them.

Unfortunately, the death of my parents caused a rift in my relationship with my daughter. She did not approve of many of our decisions. She was not happy that we hired an estate-sale company to handle selling the property inside the home. She wanted to help us handle it ourselves. However, she really had no idea of the magnitude of the work that would entail, nor the hours of labor needed to pull off the sale, nor the physical work involved and people needed to pack up and load and move every item left unsold (and there was a lot) and take it somewhere else to be sold at auction. She wanted to take some of the property to sell for her own monetary gain, but we signed a contract and couldn't allow her to do that. I gave her several opportunities to take things she wanted with my sister's approval, and she did take what she wanted to keep.

Then she complained, when she and Brody came to the estate sale, that she had to pay for the Halloween decorations and a few other items. I explained to her that the decorations were Jim's and we could only keep items that belonged to my mother.

Jessica was also upset that Mom's ashes sat in my living room for so long. To her that was a sign we didn't care if we laid her to rest. She was wrong about that.

Unfortunately, my daughter was mad about most everything we did and posted much of her anger and outrage on her Facebook page.

It was extremely difficult to deal with the constant barrage of negativity coming from her during what felt like the fight of my life. I felt attacked left and right about decisions that were not mine to make alone. I had dealt with the behavior driven by her borderline personality disorder for much of her life. I'd dealt with it while under the stress of my husband's anger and demands that I not be manipulated by her—so that I could put his needs first. I had dealt with it while I had custody of her son as an infant and then again as a five-year-old when she was not capable of caring for him. I dealt with it while dealing with the stress of my son's mental health disorders.

But this was different. This time I was being personally attacked and blamed for everything from hiring attorneys so quickly to how we sold the property to not helping Mom enough to not burying her ashes quickly enough. Accused of only caring about money. It went on and on. I felt bombarded with Jessica's hate-filled anger. All the while I was continuing to give her monetary support for their rent, food, gas and for medical needs for my grandkids. I can see now that I just wanted to take the easy road so I didn't have to fight with her. That was my part and I take responsibility for not making her learn how to stand on her own two feet. It wasn't helping to support her the way I did. I now wish I had handled it differently. Another growth opportunity that I understood a little bit late in life.

During that time she and her husband were having marital problems. One evening she had a breakdown. She had dropped the kids off at my house, and when she left, she immediately started sending me text messages that she was going to kill herself. I ended up calling the police for their help and reporting her threats. They tried to trace her cell phone but couldn't find her. I never really believed she was going to kill herself but I had to do something. I kept insisting to her that she needed to be hospitalized. She was adamant that she didn't need it. In fact, when I talked to her the day after this happened, she told me she was just having a bad day, that it wasn't a big deal. I told her that wasn't going to fly with me, that her family deserved a healthy, whole and stable mother. I told her I would have to cut her off physically and emotionally until she got that help. She did finally get help when she was committed to an inpatient rehab hospital. While she was away I helped her husband take care of the kids so he could go to work.

She was at the hospital for a week and when she came out, she informed me that her counselor helped her to understand that I was to blame for her personality disorder and that I probably had it myself. She accused me of damaging her son, who I'd had custody of for much of his life, saying that's why he had so many problems. I finally had to cut her out of my life, knowing that she would keep me from seeing my grandchildren as punishment. It was just too much. I couldn't deal with one more attack or criticism. I was done and I mean *done.*

Months later, she did let me see my grandkids. She said it was because they missed me so much and kept asking about me. I love my daughter, and I have bent over backwards trying to help her and her family, but it was time to stop. It was time for me to learn the lesson that would not go away. I knew the lesson would keep coming back until "I" changed. All this time I was waiting for her to change, when I was the one who had to stop supporting her and back off completely. They had to learn how to deal with their own problems without me.

Brody was obviously suffering greatly from his family's dysfunction. He was in eighth grade and had poor grades and poor attendance in school. He had been telling his mother he wanted to live with me, she refused to let him. By ninth grade I could see he needed help.

CHAPTER 18

Job Elimination

I said earlier that I had been on leave of absence to have surgery for a heel spur but I didn't mention I had the surgery on both feet. When Mom died, it was three weeks after surgery on the first foot so I was only dealing with recovering from that surgery. Six weeks after the first surgery, I had the same surgery on my other foot. I used my short-term disability and I was to return to work after three months, allowing me six weeks of recovery after each surgery.

I had worked for an internationally known company for fourteen years as a paralegal in their litigation department. I was to return on November 7 but was delayed a week because of an infection. The day before I was to return to work, I received a letter from my boss stating my position was being eliminated and there was no need to return.

What? But how? Why?

I realized I'd stayed out thirteen weeks, one week past the twelve weeks protected by my Family Medical Leave. My boss had to reduce his budget and I was going to be the first casualty.

They were giving me severance pay, with two months' notice, meaning I would be paid for much of the next year. Even so I was shell-shocked, disoriented, and felt sucker-punched. How could this be happening? My whole world had fallen apart in the last eighteen months. Nothing, and I mean *nothing*, was the same. I felt as if I had lost everything. How could anyone be so unlucky, one thing after another until there's nothing left? It was so surreal…my parents were gone, my husband was gone, my precious loving dogs, and now my job—all gone.

What was I going to do? I suddenly had this blank slate in front of me. It felt as though I was going to have to start my life over from the beginning. I kept hoping it was all just a bad dream, but it was real.

I didn't know what to do other than just keep putting one foot in front of the other and keep doing the next right thing or the next thing right. I wanted to have faith in that saying "When one door closes, another door opens." I wanted to have faith that my God, my Creator, knew what he was doing and I just needed to let him guide me to the next journey in my life. I knew something out there was waiting for me to find it. I needed to be open to listening for it and I would find it if I paid very close attention.

I was truly grateful for having a therapist who helped me get through all the devastation and, believe me, I relied on her heavily. My emotions were so up and down. I wanted so badly to feel normal and to deal with only normal life challenges. At the same time, I don't think I had ever really felt normal and couldn't tell you what "normal" challenges even looked like. I was really grateful that I didn't consider drinking during these events, because I knew at that point that it wasn't the answer to any of my problems and would have only made things worse.

I became pretty reclusive and didn't do much and didn't want to be around people. I went to several AA conferences, but only because a friend was encouraging me to go with her, to get me out of the house and with people. I tried to stay connected to a few people who kept checking on me but I wasn't really doing much to help myself at all. I fought bouts of depression and sadness. I often felt like a victim and frequently had my own little pity party (to my daughter's disgust). I often thought about how my mother would never let me feel sorry for myself as a kid, but she was dead now and I wanted to feel sorry for myself...I deserved it, didn't I? If anyone deserved it—by golly—it was me.

I was really glad when we finally got the estate fight behind us; gradually I was able to crawl out of my pity pot and move forward to my next journey in life.

Flash forward to the moment I knew I had to write this book, that moment sitting on that screen porch at Mom's house, reminiscing about the wonderful times we had laughing and talking and being silly while enjoying being together; I'd never imagined that house would be ours and obviously never imagined Mom would be brutally murdered there. Jim had bought a nice new double-decker dock the summer before the murder. I was looking out over that dock thinking about how crazy it was that my sisters and I had just put the house on the market and that I had no idea how things were going to go from there. I was hoping that whatever the future held, it would be as pleasant as the view I had looking out over that cove and the fleeting peacefulness I felt at that moment. I thought for sure the run of bad luck was over and that maybe now I could have time to heal and grieve her death. But it wasn't over yet. I barely had time to catch my breath before I was to face my next traumatic event.

CHAPTER 19

"You don't think I'll do it?"

I told you earlier my son had some mental health problems. He came to live with me four months before the murder, he was now thirty-five years old and had just been paroled out of prison with two years remaining of his sentence for drug-related charges. Mitchell was stable and doing well for the first nine months he lived with me. He enrolled in online classes in college, did construction and landscape work on my yard, and completed some much needed handyman repairs on my house—he was skillful with these types of things. He also helped by cooking for me and cleaning the house when I was totally down due to the foot surgeries.

He seemed really committed to changing his life and getting it together. We were getting along and enjoying each other's company. We hadn't had that in years and it felt good to share the space and have a positive, enjoyable relationship in which he could actually help me instead of the other way around. He had always wanted to be a DJ and

I helped him purchase some equipment, a Pioneer Digital DJ-SR, and Numark, Mixtrack Pro 2. He had purchased a lap top and software. He enjoyed mixing tracks and uploading them on SoundCloud for his friends to hear. I think he must have been fairly good at it. He started to get a little excited that he might be able to play at a few events. Mitchell had always been very talented and could play guitar really well. (His father had given him numerous guitars over the years but Mitchell was so unstable that he'd lost them all.)

Then in December 2013, something happened that triggered his mental health issues. He started trying to get accepted into the DJ clubs and communities which are recognized across the US. He wanted other DJs to hear the music tracks he had posted. He started to get some positive feedback from those other DJs and then started to obsess on the idea that he could make money playing music. Soon his entire focus was on doing this DJ thing.

I was worried that being a DJ at events would not be a good environment for him because they were Rave-like events. I cautioned him it was a bad idea to get back into the Rave scene. He had previously been very involved in the Atlanta Rave scene and he agreed with me about it not being a good environment. When I helped him get the equipment, I thought he was just going to mix tracks, I wasn't anticipating him trying become a paid DJ.

Then he had a serious falling out and bad experiences with the group of musicians who DJ at events, and it really hurt him emotionally. These DJs have a club and you have to be elected to be a member. They help and support people they think are good DJs and blackball the ones they think are bad, only it's done in a very aggressive and harmful way, or at least it seemed that way to me, looking in from the outside. The club is national, so DJs all over the US know who is who. I can see how that would be helpful from a local standpoint in case a club doesn't pay the DJ the agreed-upon amount. Then all the other DJs know not to play there.

As Mitchell became more frustrated that things weren't going the way he hoped they would, the battle with the club members became very destructive. My son took it quite personally and reacted with revengeful actions and attitude. He came back at them on social media and via private messages in a threatening and aggressive way. The stress caused him to spiral downward; and the pressure of this backbiting and power struggle brought on anxiety, paranoia and delusions, which resulted eventually in a complete mental breakdown and psychosis.

He couldn't handle his online school anymore so he quit. And even though I was getting around on my feet a lot better, I still could have used some help; but he stopped helping out around the house as much. I had told him before the spiraling down that he could have some friends over for a party at our house that Christmas. He planned the party, but he was a no-show as the host for it.

I knew things were going downhill fast. He started snapping at me and being rude and belligerent. During January, I was trying to get his tooth fixed (he had a broken front tooth) hoping it would help him feel better, but that didn't happen. He became severely delusional, talked about seeing things that weren't there, and accused me of secretly videotaping him in his room and selling the video online. He then started talking about the illuminati…again. The idea that I'm part of the illuminati and I control him remotely seems to surface whenever he gets delusional.

Once he became agitated and threatening, he was soon in a full-blown psychotic break. I knew he needed help. I called his parole officer begging for help. I told him something bad was going to happen, but he told me there was nothing he could do. Maddening—what's the point of the parole officer if they can't even help the person they are supposed to be watching and helping to stay out of trouble?

I called the mental health mobile crisis team to come out to my house and was sure my son would be involuntarily committed. After they arrived and he started talking about aliens and other obvious delusions, all they did was refer him to the Cobb County Mental Health Department.

I took him to Cobb County Mental Health. After four days in a row of going early to get a place in line to be seen (but he wasn't), he finally got a completely useless evaluation after a fifteen-minute interview and got two useless prescriptions. The interview was useless because he was clearly psychotic (something my therapist determined in fifteen minutes) and that psychiatrist had no information about his behavior or history beyond what he saw at that moment and sent him on his way. I filled the prescriptions and hoped for the best. The pills did absolutely nothing to help him, which did not surprise my therapist when I told her what they'd prescribed. The whole experience at the Mental Health Department left my son thinking that all the trouble we had been through to get him some help had been pointless. I had to agree with him;

we both left that day feeling our experience with the county Mental Health Department was a complete waste of time—mainly due to the fifteen-minute assessment—leaving us nowhere else to turn.

It was unbelievably frustrating. I cold-called psychiatrists' offices—they could see him in two weeks or a month. Even my son knew he needed help, and he wanted help. Unfortunately, not enough to go to the ER for an evaluation, which I believe even he probably regretted in hindsight.

Then, the day after Valentine's Day, he appeared to be much more agitated. He was glaring at me every time he walked by me. He was visibly restless, distressed and disturbed; I knew he needed to leave my house. He went to a neighbor's house and had a few beers and I told him he needed to find a place to go, that I would take him anywhere—but he had to go because I was starting to feel unsafe. He had never been violent with me, so I had no obvious reason to think he would hurt me. But I was feeling uneasy and uncomfortable.

Let me describe the layout of my house to help you picture my environment. My house has three levels. It's a log home in a neighborhood, but it is secluded, away from other homes and in the woods, with a very long gravel driveway from the street. The street is not visible from the front porch. The kitchen, which is open to the great room, the guest suite and front porch are on the middle floor; a bedroom, den and garage are on the ground floor; another bedroom and bathroom are on the top floor. A tall set of steep stairs off the front porch goes down to the ground level.

Around 6:00 in the evening, while making something to eat, Mitchell told me he was waiting for someone to call him back. He thought he could go to her house. He said he was only going somewhere he felt safe. I indicated that was fine.

While he was eating at the kitchen bar, I said something—I don't remember what—and Mitchell had a psychotic break. He completely lost control and threw his steak knife across the room and then picked it up and came at me with it. He said, "I'm going to kill you." I was sitting in a chair in the adjoining great room, only about fifteen feet from the kitchen bar where he'd been eating, and his attack was quick and caught me off guard so I didn't have time to react or get up from the chair.

He quickly ran back into the kitchen to the butcher block and grabbed two butcher knives, each about eight inches long, came over to the chair I was sitting in, leaned over me with a butcher knife in each hand and started to scream at me. I was scared and stunned in shock and disbelief. I was frozen in fear and couldn't grasp the gravity of what was happening at that moment of intense horror. Moreover, I was still recovering from foot surgery, even though it had been four months since my second-foot surgery. I was moving slowly.

His face was beet red and the anger was obvious—his eyes seemed to be bulging out of their sockets and were glazed over and dilated. He started talking crazy, threatening to kill himself and take me with him. He said he knew I was trying to kill him but he was going to kill me first. He said he had even posted it on his Facebook page a few days earlier, telling people if anything happened to him, I did it. He was jabbing those knives down towards my shoulders with each hand, stopping just before they entered my body. He kept screaming in a manic rage, "You don't think I'll do it?"

I did believe him. I saw the look in his eyes, and he was completely gone—insane. I really believed I was about to die. All I could think was *How are my sisters going to be able to live with another murder/suicide?* I started crying and begging him to stop. After several minutes of stabbing at me (without penetrating) went by, he put both knives in one hand and started spitting on me and telling me how terrible I was and how I deserved to die. I begged him to stop and I started to quietly pray.

Then he put the knives on a table next to my chair and started to punch me about the head with his fist. He continued spitting on me and hitting me on the head with his fist while I sat still in my chair and just took it. After about thirty minutes of this ranting, screaming, spitting and threatening, he tried to force me upstairs to my bedroom, which has no doors to the outside. I refused to go up there and tried to redirect him from thinking about my refusal by asking to use the bathroom. He let me go to the bathroom, but he followed me and made me leave the door open while he stood outside, close to the door.

Mitchell had taken my cell phone earlier. I learned later that while I was using the bathroom he'd started collecting all the handheld landline phones (there were two in close proximity to the bathroom) on that floor. He had put them in the pockets of his army coat. When I came out, he said he wasn't going to hurt me that I should calm down. I wanted out of the house. I told him I wanted to go out on the porch; he refused but I went out there anyway. Even though my house is very secluded, I hoped that if I could get outside someone might hear me if I screamed. My son came out to the porch with the butcher knives in his hands. He said if I screamed he would kill me. He said he just wanted to talk to me and that I was going to listen to him. For what felt like hours, he told me his life story, much of which was from his delusional perspective. He recalled numerous situations when he had used drugs. He believed his father and I didn't help him enough, accusing us of failing him. He was angry with James for the way he treated him throughout our marriage and the way he treated me. His anger towards James was understandable; however, Mitchell didn't treat James with any respect either. Mitchell went on expressing his story to me in a frantic and unsettled frame of mind while I was wrapped up in a blanket outside in the cold, quietly sobbing. I just let him talk because I suspected he needed to let out all the things causing his fury.

When he finished, he had calmed down quite a bit and was relaxed enough to realize what he had done. He became extremely distraught. We went back inside and he was shaking his head back and forth, saying he couldn't and wouldn't go back to prison. He talked about how he wished he had a gun so he could shoot himself right then.

Even after what had just happened, I felt sorry for him and I felt the worst had passed. I thought that if I could just get him to leave, we could get past that desperate moment when he realized how much more serious things had now become for him.

So I told him to take my car (even though he didn't have a driver's license) and tried to get him to leave. I swore I wouldn't call the police. It took some convincing, but he finally went downstairs. He hid all the phones somewhere, got in my car and drove off.

CHAPTER 20

Police Custody and Containment

I immediately went outside onto my front-porch deck and leaned over the rails and threw up. I was shaking and shivering and in severe shock. I went back inside, trying to get warm and to stop shaking. I couldn't think or breathe and my stomach was turning over and over. I ran outside and threw up again. After making sure all my doors were locked, I made myself sit down and try to get calm. I wrapped a blanket around me. I couldn't process what had just happened—it was already starting to be a blur and I couldn't focus. I started thinking about my mom and how she must have felt just before she was shot and how I must have felt the same fear she did. It was a moment I will never forget. I knew I had just survived a life-threatening situation and I really could not grasp the complete severity of it at that moment.

I eventually stopped shivering and must have dozed off from shock and sheer emotional exhaustion. I woke up around 3:00 a.m. I hadn't even been able to go downstairs and find the phones yet. I considered not calling the police because the thought of doing so was extremely traumatic. I knew it meant my son would be arrested and prosecuted, there would be a trial, and I would have to testify. At that moment I was so overwhelmed I couldn't even think about it. Slowly I got up and checked the doors, making sure again that they were locked. I went downstairs, found the phones and checked the doors, ensuring they were locked.

When I went upstairs, I began to get really nervous. Was he really gone? Did he leave the subdivision? Did he hide somewhere close, just to come back and hurt me? Is he going to come back during the night…in the morning…tomorrow? I jumped at every noise, and every light outside made me nervous. I had another vehicle in the driveway and started thinking he could be hiding in it, waiting for me to go outside and get in that car. It was horrible. I knew it was post-traumatic stress but what I didn't know was how long it was going to last.

I realized I just couldn't live every moment of my life worrying about him coming back to hurt me, and I couldn't put myself at that kind of risk. So I decided to call the police and I told them what happened. They took pictures of the swelling on my head and the marks on my face from being punched. They took pictures of the butcher knives, which he'd left on the front porch. One officer told me he was going to press charges against my son, meaning I didn't have to. They stayed for several hours and watched the house outside until the end of their shift because they wanted to make sure my son didn't come back.

Three days later, Mitchell called to say that he had found someone who would drive my car back to me. By a strange coincidence, the police knocked on my door while I was waiting for my car to arrive. They had a warrant to arrest my son. It wasn't the same officers who had initially answered my call and pressed charges for me. They didn't have the police report of what had happened days earlier; they were just executing the warrant. I explained that Mitchell wasn't there, that I had not seen him since the night of the incident. Although I didn't know where he was, I felt that the person he had asked to return my car might be able to help once they arrived. I figured the officers would just leave; but, instead, they decided to wait for the person to return my car. They thought there may be a chance my son would be with them, because someone had to follow behind that person to take them home.

I have a very long driveway and I'm in a cul-de-sac that you can't see from the house. I didn't know what the police were planning to do, but they must have thought it was a volatile situation and wanted him arrested. When the person driving my car pulled in my driveway, about three police vehicles pulled up on the car, and officers got out with their rifles drawn and pointing at the driver, demanding she get out and get on the ground. I didn't even know this was happening— my neighbors told me about it afterwards.

I found out later that the poor woman driving my car had *no* idea what was happening then or what had happened a few days prior. My son had not told her anything. She thought she was simply helping me get my car back. We had met several times before. She told the police that my son was at her address, in another county. The police called that county and sent the warrant to her county jurisdiction. They had him in custody within thirty minutes. I was both shocked that they went to such extremes to get him in custody and relieved that I didn't have to worry about him coming back. It was a moment of mixed emotions. It was a horrendous feeling with the flash realization of how ill he was. But I was glad he was off the street so he couldn't hurt himself or anyone else. I really felt sorry for him, that the situation had gotten so life threatening for both of us.

When the police called and let me know Mitchell was in custody, I asked what the charges were. He was charged with aggravated assault, false imprisonment, and battery—two felonies and one misdemeanor. His parole was revoked shortly thereafter and he was sent back to prison to serve out the remaining two years left on his sentence. He'd already had several felony convictions, all related to either being on drugs or distributing them.

My son has since admitted how wrong what he did was, claiming he was delusional and psychotic, which I do believe. He has shown remorse and has begged for my forgiveness. He has written me numerous letters of apology, saying he prays that I can forgive him. The truth is that he is my first-born child, my son—and I know he is mentally ill. I will always love him. I have forgiven him because it's better for me not to get stuck in resentment. I pray he will find his path in life that will bring him happiness. This is my prayer for him: It's never too late, my dearest son, to find the place you belong that will bring you peace.

In May of 2015 his case was disposed. They dropped the aggravated assault charge at my request and he pled to the other two charges. He was sentenced to five years and can be paroled in 2016. I don't really believe continued incarceration is what he needs, because he's not getting the kind of mental health support I believe he really needs. Between his past drug addiction and mental health issues, he needs long-term treatment to find the right combination of medications to remain stabilized. He won't get that while he's locked up. If his illness isn't addressed, he'll just get out again and re-offend. It's a vicious cycle because the system isn't set up to really help the mentally ill population. It's very sad and frustrating and feels like a broken record, playing the same thing over and over again. But anything is possible and I hope he gets another chance to make it in the world.

I have to keep reminding myself that his mental illness caused his actions and that it wasn't really "my son" who attacked me. If he had cancer, there wouldn't be a stigma. But mental illness carries a stigma. And it's impossible to know where the person's stability line stops and the instability line begins. How can you tell when a person crosses the line between sane and insane? I guess the answer is, you can't always tell.

I pray that someday systems are put in place, especially in my state, to truly treat the mentally ill. Systems that actually help those who suffer and that help their family members.

CHAPTER 21

A Time for Healing

Following this traumatic event, my therapist told me I was suffering from Post-Traumatic Stress Disorder (PTSD). I knew I had to surround myself with positive thoughts and energy as much as possible. I knew I had to back away from my daughter until some healing occurred in our relationship. It was the summer of 2014 (four months after the attack) and things were not going well between my daughter and her husband. They were dealing with several crises in their relationship that summer, one occurred while I was vacationing in Denver with my sisters. Jessica called and told me what had happened and she said she just "needed her mommy." I noticed that to her I was either the best mom in the world or the worst mom ever; mostly it depended on me doing or not doing what she wanted me to do. We have had times in our relationship where we were happy and loving, when she was supportive, grateful and appreciated my support. But things started to go bad after my divorce from James and it only got worse from there. Brody had some serious problems at home and at school during the fall of his ninth grade. She didn't want any input from me about it. Eventually, these disagreements made it necessary for me to stop communicating with her completely. Her energy was sucking the life out of me. I was trying to move forward and shift my thoughts to something positive and uplifting.

I found myself at the end of 2014 alone, realizing my slate had been wiped clean of most of responsibilities. I could do anything and go anywhere I wanted to because no one was depending on me but my dogs. By that time I had two new miniature Australian shepherds, Baxter and Bella, who kept me company and loved on me all the time.

I was looking for a job, but afraid my career in the legal field was over and that no one in my field would hire me at age sixty. I had gotten only two job interviews and I felt the universe telling me it was time to head in another direction.

I started searching for the missing pieces and looking for the right actions to take that would make me happy. I needed to find a sense of well-being, to feel worthy of being loved and supported. I know that happiness is an "inside job" and I can't rely on people, places and things to fill a void in my heart and soul. Some people look outside themselves to find that person or situation to make them happy and content with life. I used to think that if I had more money, more love, a nicer car, or if I weighed less or could travel anywhere in the world, that sort of thing, I would be happy. Now I believe that having more of these things could be fun and make me more comfortable, but—here's what I mean by "inside job"—true happiness comes from knowing we are exactly who we're meant to be, the way God made us. I had always believed I am a child of

God and person of worth. That God loves me as I am. So why then is it so hard to feel worthy of being loved? Something was missing inside my heart; I needed to probe and explore.

I knew I needed to find a new community, new friends and a positive place with positive energy where I felt safe and could find peace and solace. So I put that thought out to the universe and I was soon invited to join the most wonderfully healing drumming circle, full of strong and powerful women whose positive energy heals me a little more every time I attend. Those women have so inspired me with calming, healing thoughts. They have touched my heart in so many ways and made me feel so welcomed in their circle. I am challenged by all the women to find my own courage to honor my strength and power, and to have faith in the belief that I am exactly where I am supposed to be in this life journey. They encouraged me to find purpose in projects I believe in and to persevere in completing them. That helped me to understand the importance of completing the writing of this book. Their support gave me the determination to complete it.

For fun, I took some lessons to learn to play the Native American flute. That was an exciting adventure for me. Over the last several years, I had lost my ability to sing the way I had all my life—not sure if my voice got out of shape from lack of use or if the change was from trauma. Whatever the reason, I missed being able to sing as I used to. Singing had been a hugely important part of my life. Playing my guitar and singing had brought me such joy and happiness. When I wasn't singing and people asked what makes me happy, I didn't know how to answer them. I certainly enjoyed listening to music, but I needed to express myself with music; it's in my blood.

With help and encouragement from a friend, I started connecting to powerful energetic healers. This is the same friend who invited me to the drumming circle. She encouraged me to attend a workshop with Bart Smyth, A Modern Day Shaman, internationally renowned shamanic healer and grand master of Tai Chi and Qigong. I attended a three-day workshop where I learned, among other things, how to read people's energies and how to recognize energy in a room. It felt as though I really connected to the energy coming off each person who sat in the hot seat as they shared with the group their hopes and dreams for life and then the things that kept them from fulfilling those hopes and dreams. It was eye-opening and enlightening, and it started me on my journey to understanding how important my energy is and how other people's energies affect my soul, my happiness and my core being. It seemed so simple, as if I should have known it all along. It was like connecting the dots that painted a picture I was seeing for the first time.

I also experienced an amazing and powerful healing during a private session with a woman named Gentle Thunder. Gentle Thunder is a musical intuitive sound healer and Grammy-nominated multi-instrumentalist from Mount Shasta, California. She was traveling towards South Georgia when a friend of hers who had been attending the drumming circle called her and invited her to come to the circle that first night I was there. I was immediately drawn to her energy and knew I wanted to explore more of who she was and what she had to offer that could help me heal from so much trauma. At that time, I felt so broken. Gentle Thunder told me she did private sessions, in which she played many instruments that "play your essence." I didn't know what that meant but I was so intrigued I booked a session with her for four days later. She came to my home and set up her instruments in my bedroom, where I lay down in my comfy bed with my warm blanket over me. She then said an opening prayer and off she went playing the most beautiful music over and around my body. It took me on a journey which, during that session, brought in my father's spirit, which I could feel immediately. That did not normally happen to me, but he was with me the whole time, telling me it was all going to be okay. Throughout the session, I had tears streaming down my face from the emotions coming out of me.

Gentle Thunder plays the beautiful grand hammer dulcimer, sixteen Native American flutes and some light percussion. She had the most amazing ocean drum. My body vibrated when she played it, though I believe my body was vibrating during the whole session. She said she would tune in to my energy and create a healing harmonic field through the music she played. She did.

When it was over, she shared her wisdom with me. She told me I could change the way I saw and told my story. I didn't understand it exactly, then, but I came to understand she meant I could see my story through a different frame or lens, from a different perspective. I've never forgotten what she said because it rang true to my core being. I believe that first session with her was the beginning of my transformation from trauma. I have taken several more musical sessions, journeys if you will, with Gentle Thunder and I am proud to call her my friend.

A few days after my first session with Gentle Thunder, she was playing at the Sunday morning "healing service" at Unity North Atlanta in Marietta. That morning I decided to go to that church for the first time, to hear Gentle Thunder play. Another friend from the drumming circle came too and we sat together and both cried throughout the service, moved by the healing energy we felt. You could just feel this high vibration of energy in that room that moved my soul. Not long after the service started, I knew I was home. I had been spending a lot of time alone, but now I wanted a new family community. The energy during that service was so moving and spiritual for me that words do not do it justice. Between Gentle Thunder's flute, the sound ministry's Tibetan bowls, the church band, the music, the prayer shawls, the Oneness blessing and the prayer chaplains, I could physically feel the energy touch my heart and soul on such a deep level that I knew it was time for me to let go of all negative thoughts and feelings that no longer serve me.

It was time to heal.

I continued to attend this church and became a member. Every service I attend gives off such positive energy and every message I hear from Reverend Richard mends a pieces of my heart every time. The message for 2015 is to live with the knowledge that "I am holy and I know it" and if I keep believing that it will manifest my worthiness and I will receive all the positive blessings intended for me. I do believe this is my truth.

The woman who hosts the drumming circle, the Earth Mother, was, at that time writing her second book. Her name is Iris Bolton and she is a well-known author, speaker and expert on suicidology, known locally and all over the US. She is an extraordinary woman and has a way of making everyone feel accepted and appreciated. As I began to get to know her, I shared with her that I had started writing a book but had never written anything before and felt a little unsure of what I was doing. I told her my story was also about loss but not just loss from suicide. That night Iris game me a copy of her first book, *My Son...My Son...*, her story of surviving her son's suicide. I read the whole book the next day. It really touched me and inspired me. She's a very eloquent writer and I'm not nearly that eloquent, but reading it let me know I was on the right track. Something in her book really stood out to me: She wrote "...the struggle is more important than the why. After a time you can let it go and not need to know anymore."

That thought intrigues me. I think the struggle is how we deal with the pain, loss and grief—whether we allow the pain to take us out or to teach us how strong we really are and how we can turn the loss into something positive in our life. I wanted to believe I could be able to completely let go of the need to know why. I said earlier that I can accept what has happened to my mother and accept that I will never know why. But is that the same as letting go of the need to know? I think to some extent I will always wonder what happened and still be able to let go of the need to know. I think I have accomplished that, at least on some level, and it allows me to move forward on my path.

CHAPTER 22

Queen of the Forest

I began to think that all of the misfortunes and heartbreaks I went through had a purpose, a lesson I'm supposed to learn. I believe that everything happens for a reason, but I've decided I don't always need to know what the reason is. I do think the lesson or the reason will be revealed to me some day, some way. Perhaps I will also find, during my grieving, the "gift" that may come from my mother's death. That's something Iris talks about in her book.

I decided that, as difficult as it was rehashing the horrible moments of those tragedies I have experienced, writing this book should be one of those projects where I needed to persevere. Even as I write it, I have to fight off the voices inside my head that make me question whether I'm a good enough writer to do my story justice. I have to stay focused on believing the universe is telling me this story will provide hope to those who have or are suffering tragic loss or losses. It must be told.

I know I am not the only person who has suffered loss, or even multiple losses, in a short period of time. But in writing my story, I can clearly see where I indulged myself, finding that little "pity pot." I said earlier in this book that I don't like to whine or complain, and I have little patience for whiners. When I read some of my writing, I hear a little bit of whining in me. But that's okay because I can see now that it's just part of the process of acceptance, healing and moving forward. My therapist tells me that people who really play the victim tend to stay in that spot and don't take any action to help themselves move past that place. She points out that I'm taking lots of action to move past that place, to not be a victim. I am making changes, finding new friends and communities, actions and activities to help me heal and find my correct path in life.

At the exact right moment in my journey, I was introduced to a new-to-me singer/songwriter, someone whose music I was meant to hear. His music was so powerful, and the lyrics were so perfect and healing for me. His name is Bob Sima (pronounced S-EYE-ma) and he lives in Annapolis, Maryland. He was invited to sing at our Sunday service. Afterwards, he did a breath workshop that I ended up attending completely by accident. I had never heard his music before but the people at the workshop knew him and his music. I was absolutely amazed by the message my heart was receiving from his music. I can only describe it as medicine for the soul. The lyrics in every song spoke to me and I cried like a baby during most of the workshop.

One of his songs truly transformed my soul. When I heard it, I knew it could help me let go of much of the hurt and pain that was holding me back from moving forward on my journey. It isn't often you hear a song lyric that carries a message you feel could help you heal. I was meant to hear his song that day, at that time and place in my journey, and it created an immediate shift in my thinking that changed everything after that.

With his permission, I include the words to his song here in hopes that if they touch you as they did me, you will be blessed and encouraged to give your story to the trees and let it go. I mean truly let it go. I have to preface this by telling you I come from a long line of tree lovers. I love trees, my father loved trees and his father loved trees. I've always thought of trees as a living, breathing part of not just the earth but of life in general. I truly hope you will buy this music, which you can find at his website.

QUEEN OF THE FOREST
© **Bob Sima Music,** *putalittlemoreloveintheworld*, released 15 March 2014

If your heart had wings and your eyes were open
Your desperate breath lets go of its hoping
And your best friend was there to hold your trembling hand

If you're bruised and battered like nothing else mattered
The last words fell like the glass that shattered
Down the hall and the echo went on and on and on

There's a grand old tree, queen of the forest
Lay it down at her roots, I swear she's got it
You don't have to carry this anymore

It's a beautiful, beautiful day to let it go
Its okay she'll never tell a soul

Of all the trees, this one she's been waiting
The winding path, deep green parading
They say your gift you'll find it where you fall

Would you cross a mighty river to sit by her moonlight
If your greatest risk was your only insight
Would you drop your worries forever there in her arms

It's a beautiful, beautiful day to let it go
It's okay she'll never tell a soul
In the gentle of her sway no one will ever know

It's the bravest of us all who recognize the need to let it go
In her branches and her leaves, your troubles floating gently on
the breeze

If your heart had wings and your eyes were open
Your desperate breath lets go of its hoping
And your best friend's there to hold your trembling hand

There's a grand old tree, queen of the forest
Lay it down at her roots, I swear she's got it
You don't have to carry this anymore

It's okay she'll never tell a soul
In the gentle of her sway no one will ever know
It's a beautiful, beautiful day to let it go...

I just happen to have a grand old tree on my own property because I live in a forest-like place. I had thought of this tree the moment I heard this song. I believe rituals have a huge place in helping people heal and feel whole. So, although I didn't have a best friend holding my hand, I knew the day had come where it was time to let go of the hurt and that I didn't have to carry that burden anymore. Then I went to that tree and gave my story to its roots. I did it because I was desperate to overcome the traumas that fought to define me as a person. I wanted to let go of the stories that kept me feeling such a low vibration, I wanted something more positive in my life. I wanted to live being surrounded with love and light, not fear.

It was the most cathartic ritual I have ever performed in my life. I envisioned that tree holding that story for me and having my back forever by never telling a soul. I knew when I gave it to the tree, I didn't have to carry it anymore. It was an extremely powerful moment in my journey. I felt as if years of hurt and pain had been lifted off my shoulders, and I could now move on and give myself real permission to let it all go and watch the leaves from that tree float away with the wind.

After that, I felt another shift in my emotional well-being. The shift raised my awareness to a new way of thinking and manifesting a life full of love, hope and positive energy. Living in a higher vibration, I began to notice how happy and blessed I felt and how every person or thing that crossed my path was put there for me to learn from.

The best way to describe what I mean by high-vibration living is what happens when we focus on love, the kind of love we feel from God. I was also believing in the law of attraction, that if we want good things to come to us, we must do good things and feel good inside. To find peace, we must find forgiveness for those who have harmed us, be compassionate, loving, and tolerant. Living with a higher state of consciousness, similar to a meditative state, can free us from stressful thoughts and feelings that make us feel and act like small and insignificant beings or like victims. I want to shine to the world because I know it will generate a feeling of wholeness inside me that others can see and feel too. I try to perceive the whole universe as part of oneself.

I believe that all life on this earth, the trees, the animals, the seas, are connected and part of God. I began to notice that any time I put something out to the universe (expressed a desire for something to come to me), the answers and resources came to me almost immediately. I started meeting people that I knew had a role in or connection to my journey and I knew these were not coincidences. I call it synchronicity. It made me realize that God is in us and we are part of God and that God is love.

After making all these connections, I noticed I was ecstatically happy. The happiness created the high vibration. I wasn't worrying about money or not having a job or what I was supposed to be doing with my life. I somehow knew it was part of a plan and I wasn't in control of it, and that was so very acceptable to me. I surrendered to the magical, mystical and spiritual rebirth that I was helping create for myself. I was totally in tune with the energy I felt from people at church and in the drumming circle and around me in general. I was feeling that high vibration all the time. I created a meditation room, filled it with various instruments—a drum, Tibetan bowls, chimes—and the music that was now the medicine for my soul. Then I surrounded myself with crystals, reading about how to work with them and feeling their energy.

I started working with a spiritual mentor, an intuitive and medium. She taught me how to call in my angels and spirit guides to ask for their help, and I see signs that they hear me and help me. For example, I asked my spirit guides to help direct me to the work I was supposed to be doing. The next day I met a person at church who started talking about how a project at her office had her very stressed out because she needed help. I told her I had experience in that area and she asked me to come the next day to talk about helping her. I ended up doing some consulting work for her that brought in a little income for me. It's just one example, but I could talk about numerous others. It sometimes feels surreal.

I received a psychic reading that helped me find the path for a new beginning. I believe I'm being led to some very exciting things and I sense why certain events have brought me to this point in my life. I can already see that the connections from what has happened in the past to what is happening in my life now have been divinely guided by God and the Universe. Now is a time for the emergence of my new self. I believe that anything I do from my heart with love I can be successful at. I am just starting to learn I have specific abilities and talents that will lead me to be of service in many ways to this planet.

One new and exciting thing I have done is to complete Reiki I training. Reiki is a Japanese technique for stress reduction and relaxation that also promotes healing. It is administered by "laying on hands" and is based on the idea that an unseen "life force energy" flows through us and is what causes us to be alive.

My goal is to strive to live every day letting go of my expectations of people, forgiving, loving and releasing that which no longer serves me. I still have a long way to go in achieving this goal on a daily basis but at least I endeavor to get there.

There's so much more to learn and I thank the Creator for all my blessings. Every Sunday in church we sing one of Karen Drucker's songs, it's sort of a chant with the words "I am so blessed, I am so blessed, I am so grateful for all that I have, I am so blessed, I am so blessed, I am so grateful, I am so blessed." I cry tears of gratitude every time I sing it because I believe it and it's overwhelming, feeling how blessed I am so deep in my soul.

I'm singing in the church choir and I'm playing guitar again. My voice is coming back and getting better. I've also been invited to sing back-up with two other singers for the recording artists who perform at our Sunday services. I sometimes sing songs of prayer at our drumming circle. It makes me so happy to bring song and music back into my life. Though I still have much work to do in getting my voice back in shape, I believe it will come back bigger and stronger than it ever was and Spirit is sending me messages that my voice will have a role in helping others heal, and that this is my life's purpose. I don't know what that means or looks like exactly but the message is strong. I just have to keep listening and it will all be manifested just the way it is supposed to be.

CHAPTER 23

A New Life

So here is my story, the good and the bad, the sad and the glad. I know I have survived the worst things I can think of happening to me short of losing my health. I do not fear death. At times during these past few years I wanted to give up when I felt I had nothing to live for, but that is wrong and not my truth. I know that the reason I'm experiencing all of this is for me to find a new path, a new life even better and more rewarding than before.

As of the middle of 2015, I am estranged from my daughter, and the courts have given me permanent custody of my grandson. He is thriving at a new school but is there every day and plays on the school's basketball team. He is very active and connected to the kids at the Y.O.U. (Youth of Unity) group at our church. It is an extremely positive environment for him and it's wonderful to see him happy there. I do get to spend time with my other two grandsons who are now six and five.

They bring me so much joy and laughter and I am very grateful for the time I have with them.

I can't say what the future holds for my relationship with Jessica, but I believe it's all unfolding exactly the way it is supposed to. She had written to the Dr. Phil show who called me and asked if I would be willing to come on the show. After much discussion with my sisters, I thought it might be a positive step towards repairing our relationship but the timing was not right and we didn't do the show.

So no matter how much hateful and negative energy consumes her, I just envision myself surrounded with light and love and a wall of protection built by my guides and angels. I will always love her. I have forgiven her and will continue to send her the same light and love that surrounds me. I pray for all my children and grandchildren and know that my father watches over all of us. I was told in a reading that my Dad is a builder in heaven and he told me he could build me anything, all I had to do was ask. So anytime I need help, I ask him and I know he's there and it brings me much comfort.

I have no doubt that the people who surround me now have been put in my path to help guide me on my journey. I look forward to finding out what comes next. I don't take anything for granted. I try to look carefully at every situation I encounter or person I meet to see what I am supposed to learn from that situation or person. Looking at life this way has definitely made me more open-minded and open to accept the blessings I was meant to receive from God and the universe. I am astounded at how much more I feel and sense the energy around me now so I try to keep myself surrounded with positive-thinking people.

A lot about this book may not seem positive: The main reason I wrote it is that I hope it will give people who have lost their loved ones, or been the victims of violence, the courage to accept what has happened to them, grieve their loss, and find a positive way to recover and heal from whatever tragedy or trauma they have experienced.

I strongly believe that all of life's challenges have been put in our path in order for us to grow and to reach or find our highest good. We have to own our mistakes and realize what we can learn from them. You may even believe there are no mistakes because we can learn as much from our failures as we can learn from our victories. The trick is to get centered, be silent, and listen to the message from the God inside you and to take the next right action. If you do that, you will find your best path. If you don't find your best path at first, keep in mind that there are no wrong paths. If you can get quiet, listen and pay attention, you will eventually feel the need to move in a different direction.

For some of you, experiencing one traumatic loss or incident could take you to the depths of despair. For most of us, it's not easy to deal with the emotions that come with losing your loved one to a violent death or to mental illness. But if you have heard anything in my story, I hope you heard a message that you can survive it. It takes time. Let yourself feel every emotion, the anger, the confusion, the denial, the sadness, hurt and pain. Don't try to cover it up with drugs or alcohol, because the grief and pain are going to get you sooner or later, one way or another. The attempts to numb yourself and push down the emotions will only drag out your misery and make you hurt longer and harder. The alcohol or drug will only delay the inevitable. Find a support group of people who have gone through what you are going through. Talk about it as often as you need. One of my negative thoughts was believing that people didn't care about my life struggles because they have their own, which meant they didn't want to hear about mine. It's true that some people don't want to hear about it, but others will find hope in your story—hope that could change their lives, or at the very least make them feel better. I can't stress this enough: Find a place where you can keep talking and sharing your feelings and emotions, ignoring them will do no good.

Take one day at a time, and find something to do that you enjoy to distract you at times from thinking about the loss, even if it's just for a day, an hour or a minute. It will get better; it will get easier. Don't distract yourself all the time and don't hold it inside—let it out, speak your truth and share the hurt for as long as it takes.

If telling my story helps you believe that you can survive one of these life events, then my sharing has accomplished my goals for this book. If you think your story will help someone, then I encourage you to pay it forward by telling your story, too, because your story is worthy of telling. Believe that.

My story is not over. Transformation is an ongoing process; it's a journey not a destination, and will continue on its path. It might even lead me to another book; you never know.

Love and light and God bless you all. And so it is…and so we let it be.

A'ho and amen!

Made in the USA
Middletown, DE
21 September 2016